Management of Manpower Training and Development

MANAGEMENT OF MANPOWER TRAINING AND DEVELOPMENT

J. M. Dewan

DISCOVERY PUBLISHING HOUSE
New Delhi-110002

Edition - 2020

ISBN: 978-81-7141-448-2

Management of Manpower Training and Development

Published by:

DISCOVERY PUBLISHING HOUSE PVT. LTD.
4383/4B, Ansari Road, Darya Ganj
New Delhi-110 002 (India)
Phone: +91-11-23279245, 23253475; 43596065
E-mail: discoverybooksindia@gmail.com
discoverypublishinghouse@gmail.com
web: www.discoverypublishinggroup.com

Printed at:
Infinity Imaging Systems
Delhi

Preface

In India considerable importance has been accorded to training in social development. Obviously while few would deny that training is essential, there is considerable doubt about its optimal contribution to development. There are complaints about the ineffectiveness of training and possible waste of resources because of the use of stereotyped and conventional methods in training which are often not set completely in tune with job requirements. On the one side there is pressure of training a large number of functionaries, on the other there is an urgent need for improving the quality of training. One of the reasons for this is that very little time is devoted to planning of a training programme. The organisation of training is based on certain assumptions which are need-based to be substituted in accordance with new concepts of training.

The rapid technological changes in today's industrial and business environment bring increasing pressure on the training functions to play a more active role in technical and professional training. Although the need is greatest and most obvious in research and development organizations whose products and services are based on advanced states of the arts, product-producing organizations also feel the increasing need to maintain an up-to-date technology. The growth of research and development departments and product development facilities is a case in point.

Technical and professional training is a widespread requirement of business organizations today.

Professional training programs in the scientific laboratory or engineering department can be found in almost every function from junior technician to chief engineer. But this requirement is spreading from the laboratory; it extends to production functions as well. Changes in production methods--numerical control, automated production control techniques, and, in fact, the introduction of computer applications to every system of the organization may be the subject for training actions in the technical professional areas.

Editor

CONTENTS

1

Manpower Training and Development

Our first task is to gain an understanding of the full process of manpower development. We can then identify what has to be done to produce a favourable development, and come to some conclusions about roles and relationships. Within this pictures the place of the training function should become clear.

We shall start by examining in outline the general case of any company whose present situation is reasonably well understood by its management, and whose future is under close scrutiny by that management. One question which is being asked concerns future manpower: are the right steps being taken to make sure that the numbers and qualities of employees are correct and to the right level? This is a question often asked by directors. They must be given an answer that does not merely state that something is being done, but that the right things are being done. How to determine the right things to do—a management responsibility.

In an ideal analytical world the manpower development work of a company would be conducted in order to include and throw light on the following.

The present company

Information is required under the following headings:

(a) The present activities and technologies, with details of machinery, equipment, processes, product volumes etc.

The current need for employes, but number and quality, to satisfy the activities and technologies.

(b) The present actual manpower, with detailed age structure, occupational details of skill and experience, employee wastage patterns and rates, organisation and hierarchies.

Thus we have a picture of what the company does, makes, etc, of how it does it, with what equipment, plant and methods; and of the manpower required, together with its ageing and wastage characteristics, and quality.

The future company

At a specified date in the future, e.g. in five years' time, the company will be different. One would like to know such things as

(a) The future activities and technologies, with details of future machinery, equipment, process and product volume.

(b) The future manpower, with details of the future organisation and hierarchies, and numbers; the distribution of skills and qualities across the organisation; the future desirable age structures.

The manpower objective and strategy

The manpower objective is to achieve the future manpower as specified. The manpower strategy will define the types of actions, in broad terms, which are to be taken in order to meet this objective. The strategy will embrace

Employee retention, redundancy and recruitment

Promotion and transfer

Education and training and job experience

Organisation development.

The manpower plans

These will provide statements of the details of action to be taken by the subsidiary manpower functions of education and training, recruitment, personnel development etc. to meet the manpower targets, and of how these actions interlock in order that the defined strategy can be pursued and the targets met.

From this point on, action is taken by the subsidiary functions and, with sufficient monitoring and co-ordination at a senior management level, the desired manpower structures and qualities emerge in the course of time. Unfortunately the situation is rarely, if ever, as simple and as clear-cut as described in this ideal picture. Manpower targets prove to be wrong; recruitment proves to be difficult: the original strategies are inappropriate. One again the personnel function is pilloried for neglecting its responsibilities, and urged to improve its manpower capability.

But is it a question of capability? Can you get the 'right' answer by being a better analyst and planner? Or are there factors and difficulties in this work which make precision illusory? We shall look more closely at the problems of the analyst.

We wish to know two things as precisely as possible. First, the details of the future manpower requirement, in quantitative and qualitative terms.

Second, we wish to know the extent to which the present manpower will contribute, at that later date, to providing the future manpower. We shall use the symbol Mp for the present manpower, in quantity and quality today. However, if all the normal processes of ageing and leaving the company continue, as one would except, the present manpower Mp will have become older and smaller, and somewhat more experienced. This older and smaller version of Mp we shall call Mc, the suffix standing for 'core', implying that there is a 'core' of employees who remain over a length of time, the rest dying or leaving the company.

We can now construct a small equation, of great significance in manpower planning. It is

Mf - Mc = Md

which reads, 'The difference between the manpower you want at a future date, (Mf), and the core of manpower you will be left with from your present strength (Mc), is the manpower you have to develop (Md) between now and that future date.' It is a commonsense equation. Its simplicity of statement must not be confused with the complexity of achievement - when one looks at essential details. We shall consider the three factors in turn.

The future manpower

This will be based, as indicated above on the trade levels, technology, and manufacturing methods of the future. The questions to be asked in the first instance are

1 What will the company be making and in what quantity?

2 Will there be the same plant with the same manning principles as today, or will there be new plant? What is known of the manning needed for it?

3 Will non-production employment, on administration, computers, research etc. be maintained , or altered?

Some management will plain to know, with precision, their plans for five or eight years hence. Some will be confident about manning requirements. But many be hesitant about both and with good reason. For any company change, any growth not yet under way, is subject to some uncertainty. This is due to the unpredictability of future markets, competition, finance, automation, take-overs and mergers-to mention a few influences. What is not yet on the drawing board or not yet building, cannot be quoted with full confidence.

Hence the manpower manager, looking for information on the operations of more than, say, two to three years in the future, may not get the precise answers he is looking for. He may even be baffled by the variety of answers he gets from managers of comparable senior responsibility, particularly on projects on which no corporate final decisions have yet been taken.

The manpower core

Fortunately the analysis leading to an estimate of core size contains one element that is unarguable—that of ageing. The analyst can predict the ages of all members of the company x years ahead (assuming them still to be alive) and can account for those who will have retired by that time. What he cannot be so confident about is employee wastage; the loss of employees who leave to join other companies. This loss rate will be dependent on a number of influence, internal and external, some of which can be analysed in greater detail, some of which cannot. If there is a general expansion in the economy there could be an increase in wastage of people leaving to take better jobs elsewhere; if the economy becomes depressed then the wastage may well reduce. A study of business cycles continue in the same pattern as in the past.

What age-structure and core-analysis will not reveal is who will leave the company, apart from those who retire. This may or may not be improvement: it is important when considering the future role of special trainee groups of technical, supervisory, executive or management type, on whose shoulders high responsibilities are to rest. These groups are especially sensitive to internal conditions and opportunities as well as to the higher paid opportunities offered by competitive companies outside.

Whilst core-analysis may produce an adequate picture of the numbers of people in any particular class, a further form of study is required to estimate the spectrum of quality of people in that class. This study, a study of human potential, may be undertaken ontwo distinctly different bases, as follows.

The first we shall call statistical That is, if, in the company's 20 years of experience, Y per cent of executive aged 30 have become competent managers at specified higher levels by the age of 37, generation by generation, then it is reasonable to suppose that this development is repeatable given that the latest batch of 30 year old is of the same generation, then it is reasonable to suppose that this development is repeatable given that the latest batch of 30 year olds is of the same general quality as before, and the that the increase in responsibilities to be carried is about the same. For example, if during a period of 20 years, of 350 executives aged 30 in junior management posts, 70 have successfully occupied middle management posts, and of these 35 have successfully occupied senior management posts, then one can say there is evidence that 10 per cent of junior managers make the grade as senior managers and 20 per cent as middle managers. A trend analysis would need to show nos significant change of type of person or type of work. This does not indicate exactly who is the manager of the future, but it does give an indication of whether the number of people of that quality will exist in the company.

The second we shall call individual assessment. In this case each person is looked at in order to find evidence that he has the character, capability and capacity for development that will enable him to carry higher responsibilities, general and/or specific, in the future. The assessment may be carried out by one or more managers, by specialists, or through the help of specially designed tests and exercises in assessment centres. There is little factual evidence of much accuracy attributable to the use of either unsophisticated or the more sophisticated techniques in industrial and commercial companies; but techniques continue to develop, and can only develop successfully if they are put to realistic practical test. Personal judgement continues to be widely used, and often preferred despite its acknowledge weakness and failures.

Returning then to the quantitative and qualitative characteristics of the future manpower core, we find that, again, there is uncertainty about the estimate of both the size and the qualitative characteristics of that core.

We now have to 'subtract' the core, Mc, from the future manpower, Mf, to tell us the size and quality of manpower that is to be developed, Md. Were Mc and Mf single precise figures produced with confidence and accuracy, the arithmetic and the ensuing target setting would be undertaken with relative ease. With Mc and Mf both uncertain, it is imperative to deal with this uncertainty sufficiently thoroughly, to produce valid manpower plans and to enable the subsidiary manpower activities to be planned with responsible confidence.

We must appreciate that whatever the uncertainty of the future, both in the environment and within the employee groups, it is unacceptable for this uncertainty to become a psychological lack of confidence in those who have to approve manpower actions, and those who have to execute them. These managers and executives should fully understand the probabilistic nature of future prediction; and they should be knowledgeable and confident about the rationale which produces the final executive decision.

One way of dealing with a number of uncertain predictions or outcomes, is to examine each outcome in turn, assess what action is required of the company in each outcome and then see what the variation of those actions is going to be. Within this range of variation of action there may be some which are practical, some of them similar.

There may be one or more actions which look impossible, or are too expensive. These will cause management to rethink their operating objectives, provided very believe that those particular outcomes are reasonable likely to occur.

Two frequently used method of analysis are based on the use of alternative scenarios and the use of sensitivity analysis. Both are used by economists ion company and national forward estimating and planning, and their use in manpower planning is increasing. An outline of their methods will suffice for this text.

Alternative scenarios

When we think of the world as having a particular level of economic activity, a particular level of employment and a particular level of technology, we are specifying and describing a 'scenario'. Against this scenario, or back cloth, we can then describe the response of our company to the influences which act on it, influences which are determined by that scenario. We can create, in our minds and paper, as many scenarios as we wish, and then estimate the company performance in each. We would not waste time examining scenarios which were, in whole or in part, unlikely to occur, and the use of alternative scenarios demands skill and discrimination in deciding how varied the chosen scenarios are to be, and how far into 'the unlikely' one needs to enquire.

The chosen scenarios might be based on the following factors

1 The economy, national and/or international may be

(a) vigorous (b) average (c) weak

2 The company's growth may be

(a) high (b)low

Thus we have six, i.e. 3 ´ 2, scenarios against which to

estimate the demand on company manpower, and against which to make propositions on the steps to be taken to provide Md, i.e. the development of manpower to deal with the company's business in each particular scenario. One of these scenarios is that chosen by the general manager for the establishment of overall corporate trading and operating objectives.

In the examination of manpower, in each scenario there will be values for Mf and for Mc appropriate to that scenario, e.g. the wastage rate will differ from scenario to scenario and will produce different manpower cores: the company's need for executives, technologists, researchers, could be higher in a time of high company growth and produce, therefore, a larger value for Mf, the manpower required in the future.

We can estimate, therefore, for each scenario, a value for Md, in numbers and types, in quantity and quality, that have to be developed during the period of time between now and that future date. We now have to propose how each development of manpower is to take place.

The development will be based in each case, on

(a) The behaviour of the core, already allowed for in our estimates, but for whom continuing developmental provisions may be required to achieve the new qualities required.

(b) The recruitment of extra personnel to achieve the planned size and the required age, grade and skill structures.

(c) The training and development of the new recruits, initially and thereafter, to achieve the qualities required.

There are four major constraints which have to be taken into account

(i) the development of individual and team capability will be based on learning through work, on-the-job exposure and instruction, movement through 'progressive' responsibilities, as well as by attendance at courses, seminars, etc. and reading. The organisation and execution of the above, particularly the job movements, must be undertaken in such a way as to allow the company's work to continue smoothly and efficiently as well as to provide suitable developmental experience for the individuals.

(ii) recruitment plans and action envisaged must be realistic, taking into account the likely state of the labour market and availability of suitable recruits in the scenario under consideration.

(iii) there will be wastage amongst those newly and recently recruited: this will probably be higher than for the existing manpower and needs separate wastage estimates.

(iv) there needs to be compatibility between the companys' plans for moving, training and progressing the career of individuals, and the interests and ambitions of those individuals. Steps must be taken to bring about pay, work and career satisfaction, as far as this is possible, for all employees both inside and outside the manpower development network of plans and programmes.

Alternative manpower development strategies

We now have, for each scenario, a strategy for manpower development. Each strategy contains a statement about

Recruitment - by number, type, work area

Transfers - into new work areas, either for or not for planned development

Promotion - into new/old work areas, either for or not for planned development

Training - by types; training objectives/ corporate objectives

And an indiction of the way that these are intended to interlock to meet the manpower requirement for that scenario. They are interdependent and contribute to a specific manpower objective. They can only be fully and professionally understood by referring to the details of, and assumptions about, the scenario itself.

Merely having a number of scenarios, each with its manpower requirement and strategy proposal, might be little more than confusing. Someone has to decide which scenarios to go for: that someone may be the general manager of the company or the managing directors. It is not the personnel manager of the manpower manager, for the scenarios must be the same as those chosen by general management for planning future company operations. Thus the choice of scenario and the 'preferred' manpower strategy is made by line management.

Account may now be taken of the future being uncertain. No one will wish to proceed on the basis that the future will precisely correspond to the one chosen scenario. It is believed, or hoped, to be the most likely one, but precautions must be taken for the occurrence of the less likely. This is achieved strategies, and comparison enables the company management to estimate the error of the preferred strategy if, in the course of events, the world follows the course of a different scenario, for which a different strategy should have been prescribed. A number of answers will then come to light to the questions

(i) What are the differences between the preferred manpower strategy and the other strategies?

(ii) Are the differences great or small, important or unimportant?

(iii) Will it be possible effectively to change from the preferred strategy to that which is required by the actual future situation?

(iv) Can contingency plans be drawn up now to deal with the changes in strategy at any point?

(v) What is the cost of pursuing a 'wrongly' chosen strategy?

(vi) Is there a substantial common element to all the strategies? If so can a 'common strategy' be defined, based on this common element, with small additional strategy items to be added to it according to which scenario is enacted? As an example, it may be possible to say that irrespective of which strategy we are considering, 42 men must definitely be upgraded to junior supervision and then add to this number 0, 3, 6, 7 extra for strategies A, B, C and D. Thus, with a well chosen common strategy one can proceed with confidence that the ultimate error is unlikely to be great—and later corrective steps may be possible in good time.

Sensitivity analysis

The selection of a common strategy is very similar to the first step insensitivity analysis. In this, a single scenario, or a single set of assumptions about the economy and the company's trading activity, is drawn up. From this the future manpower requirement (Mf) and the manpower development to be undertaken (Md) may be estimated, as in the instances above. From this a single manpower strategy is devised, plus action plans.

Any likely variation in, for example, company growth, or the availability of external recruits, which are different from the figure put into the main calculations are then, in further calculations, given greater or lesser values, and the change in the resulting manpower requirement is calculated. Thus, for example, having assumed an executive wastage rate of 7.2 per cent per unman for the main calculation, we answer the question 'what if it is 10 per cent' by replacing the 7.2 by 10 per cent in the computation. The impact of this on the creation of vacancies, on internal movement and promotion requirements and on external recruitment requirements will be calculable. One will see precisely how sensitive the company's manpower is to variations in executive wastage. The manpower plans may have to be amended if it is shown that the company is seriously sensitive to variation in any one or more such factors.

2

Manpower Planning Systems

Manpower planning is the process of making decisions regarding the acquisition and utilization of human resources. In particular, the manpower plan focuses on an analysis of the organization's objectives and the plan for acquiring resources to meet these objectives. The organization's objectives and the resources acquisition process are analyzed in terms of the role that human resources plan in achieving organizational goals.

Planning

Planning is often considered "formal decision making" in the sense that it involves " deciding in advance what to do, how to do it and who is to do it." It involves a determination of objectives to be accomplished at some future date, an assessment of whether existing organizational policies, programs, and procedures are sufficient to accomplish the objectives, a review of alternative approaches to accomplishing objectives, and the organization of resources to implement the alternative chosen.

Strategic planning is the process of allocating resources into new areas whether they be in new product markets, geographical areas, or into new production processes in an effort to more effectively accomplish the goals of the organization. Strategic decisions in organizations are made on a continuous basis, sometimes systematically using sophisticated planning techniques, and sometimes without much involvement in formal processes. The emphasis of this chapter is on the need for a systematic approach to manpower planning and a general model of a manpower plan.

A narrower definition of planning focuses simply on the "how to do" and "when to do" portion of the objectives. Here, laying out a course of action to be followed is considered planning. It is assumed objectives have been identified in a previous step and that making task assignments to accomplish the plan will occur in a later step.

For our purposes, we will use the broader definition of planning since we are concerned with insuring that a given plan is objective oriented that it does indeed focus on the accomplishment of a given goal or end result and that some time sequencing in carrying out the plan is specified. However, we will not be as concerned with making specific task assignments to carry out the plan.

Manpower planning is the sum total of the plans formulated for the recruiting, screening, compensation, training, job structure, promotion, and work rules of an organizations' human resources. It "is a process designed to translate the corporate or institutional plans and objectives into future quantitative and qualitative manpower requirements, together with plans to fulfill those requirements over both the shorter and longer terms, through manpower utilization, human resource development, employment and recruiting, and manpower information systems,"

The emphasis in this definition is on structuring plans to carry out what are considered to be the traditional personnel management functions of hiring, training, compensation, and promotion.

Macro-micro distinction

Manpower planning is done on a national level primarily by the central government aided by the states. This type of planning has a different focus from the manpower planning done by an individual organization. National manpower planning, or *macro* manpower planning, involves the specification of national manpower objectives and programs for their accomplishment. It usually involves federal agencies, such as the Department of Labour, particularly, the Employment and Training Administration, and certain agencies within the Department of Health, Education and Welfare. However, other national organizations, such as the Brookings Institution, are also involved in macro manpower planning activities.

Manpower plans at the national level change as the priorities of a particular Congress and/or administration change. For example, under Presidents Kennedy and Johnson a great deal of effort and funds were spent to develop manpower plans to deal with specific manpower problems. Programs were established for remedial education and skill training, mobility benefits, equal employment opportunity, and labor market information system. Most of these programs in this period were directed at improving the employment relationship of minorities and disadvantaged groups in keeping with the philosophy of the New Frontier of the Kennedy administration and the Great Society Program of the Johnson administration.

However, during the Nixon administration manpower priorities changed. Increased emphasis was given to improving the employment situation of veterans and in improving the already existing federal offices, such as the federal-state Bureause of Employment, to help all levels of manpower. The emphasis on programs for the disadvantaged and minorities was reduced.

The Nixon administration also decentralized the ational manpower planning effort by establishing egional offices throughout the nation and, through the evenue sharing program, by asking each state to handle he manpower planning function for the state. Even hough the decentralization process has achieved only imited success, the responsibility for national manpower lanning has shifted from a centralized federal overnment in Washington to decentralized regional nanpower offices and individual state governments.

Micro manpower planning involves the planning an rganization does for the acquisition and utilization of its nanpower. As seen in our definition of manpower lanning, this is the focus we use in our book. However, his does not mean that macro manpower planning, vhether it be done solely by the federal government or ointly by the federal government and the states, has an nsignificant impact on micro manpower planning. For xample, when federal programs were established to mprove the employment opportunities for the so called 'hard-core" unemployed, individual organizations were sked to commit extra resources and to develop nanpower plans that included programs for recruiting, raining, and employing these individuals.

Often federal programs will stimulate an rganization to do manpower planning that did little if ny manpower planning in the past. For example, overnment federal law and programs dealings with equal employment opportunity and affirmative action caused many organizations to review their present manpower planning process. The thrust of affirmative action planning involves the development of an organizational plan to recruit, train, and employ more members of minorities and women than are presently employed by the organization. As organizations review the number of employees presently employed in various positions and develop plans to replace these employees to ensure that minorities are being recruited, they usually end up doing a comprehensive review of their total manpower planning system.

For example, an organization may decide to set up a skills bank or skills inventory of all minority and women employees currently employed to insure that they will be considered for future promotion when positions become vacant. As they begin setting up such a skills bank for minorities, they soon realize that this would be a good idea for all employees, whether white or black, male or female. Thus, they are on the way to developing a complete manpower or human resource information system for all employees, which is a critical aspect of manpower planning.

Therefore, the macro manpower planning done on the national level affects the micro manpower planning done by an individual organization. However, there are other aspects of the macro environment, besides national manpower planning, which also affect, in a major way, the micro manpower planning function.

The macro environment of manpower planning

Some major components of an organizations' macro environment. These are the cultural values and norms, social institutions, legal environment, product/service demand, technology, and human resource mix. Each of these components has an impact on the manpower planning system of an organization.

Product/service demand mix

Forecasted demand for an organizations' product/service serve as the primary basis for an organization's manpower plan. As demand for an organizations' product or service increases substantially, people are added to the organization, usually at all occupational levels. As demand decreases, people are usually at all occupational levels. As demand decreases, people are usually laid off or discharged at all levels,. even though individuals at lower occupational levels are usually released first.

Since most organizations have an objective of growth, and since national economic policy is one of growth, the predominant influence of product/service demand forecasts is one of providing additional manpower for the organization as it grows. Therefore, one function of the manpower plan is to ensure that the desired number of people with appropriate skills and abilities are available for appropriate jobs and occupations in the organizations as the demand for the organization's product/service increases.

However, the manpower plan also make provision for organizational manpower decisions for periods or retrenchment, such as during an economic recession. Some organizations, for example, lay off unskilled workers first during a recession rather than skilled, professional, or managerial employees. The rational here is that the unskilled employee is the easiest to replace during an economic growth period. Other organizations tend to lay off employees regardless of skill during a downturn in activity. Aerospace and defense contractors, for example, typically lay off high skilled supervisors, engineers, and technicians along with unskilled and semi-skilled employees during a business downturn.

Still other organizations will reduce the work hour of all employees rather than lay off anyone during a recession. For example, many organizations in Japan will go to a reduced work-week and a cut in wages and salary for all employees, including managers, rather than to lay people off during a business downturn. Thi reflects the paternalistic managerial philosophy of man Japanese organizations.

Governmental agencies typically reduce budgets fc the next fiscal year and rely on normal attrition to reduc the workforce rather than laying off people durin periods of economic downturn. As people retire or qui they are replaced until economic conditions improve.

Whatever the particular policy of an organizatio during periods of economic recession, it needs to b clearly spelled out and implemented in makin manpower decisions. Going through the process o formulating a manpower plan that thoroughly consider the effects of economic recession as well as economi growth often provides many unnoticed opportunities fo an organization.

For example, some organizations actually adc people in certain highly skilled occupational position during a recession, for it is during this time that ar organization can bring on board skilled people whc aren't available during normal business activity except a a very high salary premium. Some companies hirec skilled engineers rather than laying them off during the 1973-74 recession because they had a wide supply tc choose from and did not have to pay a premium Assuming these engineering skills would be needed when to pay economic picked up, these companies made a wise choice since they obtained skilled manpower at lower salaries than during normal periods. Some colleges and universities also followed this policy during the 1973-74 recession to attract top faculty who would otherwise not be available at the salary these colleges could offer.

Thus, one major function of the manpower plan is to

provide an orderly system to add employees to the organization during periods of economic growth and to specify procedures to be followed during periods of economic recession or organizational retrenchment. A good manpower plan allows organizations to smooth out the hiring process so that variations in hiring are not widely divergent from year to year, depending upon market conditions. Organizations without a good manpower plan often find that they hire large numbers of employees one year only to lay them all of the following year.

The key to an effective manpower plan that recognizes the effect of economic conditions is adequate forecasting of these conditions as well as the organization's product/service mix as economic conditions change. An organization should not be at the mercy of economic conditions, but should forecast and develop well-conceived manpower plans is advance of changing conditions.

Changing technology

Technological changes have a profound impact on an organizations' manpower plan. As technology changes, the skills required in particular occupations change. New occupations are created, and old ones cease to exist. The trend over the last fifty years has been to upgrade the skills required in most jobs in our economy. Many of the unskilled jobs, particularly those involving heavy labor, have been eliminated. Labor demand in some skilled occupations has also been eliminated or significantly reduced. We are all familiar with the plight of the blacksmith.

The composition of many skilled jobs change as technology changes. Often the skill components are broken down into separate jobs, which can be performed by semi-skilled workers. For example, the introduction of a highly automated assembly line into the typical manufacturing operations of a company in the 1950s often broke up skilled jobs into several separate jobs requiring lesser skills. These jobs would be routinely performed by workers during the course of a normal day's work on the assembly lines and many became boring because of their repetitiveness.

Another aspect of a technological change is that, while it often eliminates unskilled jobs involving physical labour, it may create semi-skilled jobs requiring repetitive mental and manual labor. The modern auto assembly line has many examples of these.

Changing technology also requires organizations to plan for changes in locating sources of manpower to insure that supplies of needed manpower will be recruited. For example, the introduction of electronic data processing into an organization often requires the organization to recruit skilled computer technicians from technical schools in which they may not have recruited previously.

A technological change often means the organization's own training program must be revised to insure that people with skills needed in the future will be available. Thus, plans have to be made that: (1) forecast future technological change and the skill needs they will create, (2) determine classroom and on-the-job training programs to fill the needs, and (3) prepare instructors, instructional material, and facilities for the training. For many significant technological changes, such as the introduction of electronic data processing, an organization may choose to do little of its own internal training but rely on formal schooling. Any internal training becomes an orientation to show how the organization use the EDP system.

Human resource skill/educational mix

The changing skill/educational mix of the human resource supply and changing technology are closely related. As technology changes to require different skills and abilities, people attempt to change their ability/skill mix to gain skills required in jobs. This matching of the skill requirements of jobs with the skills of people in the work force has been the underlying thrust of government manpower policy. Training and development programs sponsored by the government were established to ensure that people, particularly the disadvantaged and minorities, would be able to secure the needed skills to compete effectively in the labor market.

The tremendous growth in secondary and two year post-secondary vocational and technical schools since 1962 was a result of federal manpower planning, which indicated a need for formal classroom training to provide the skilled work force needed in today's highly technological society. Many regions of the country now have area vocational schools, and many students who might have not gone to college, now receive two years of post-secondary technical training in such fields as electronics, computer technology, aviation technology, automotive mechanics, and the applied medical fields.

When the human resource educational/skill mix differs significantly from the skills required by employers, manpower shortages develop. Employers have jobs open but cannot find people with the skills demand ed. Many people want jobs but are hired because they do not have needed skills. This mismatch between job skill requirements and the skills of the labor force can have a serious negative impact on the economy of a society. For example, in the late 1960s, we had a national unemployment rate under 4.0 percent for 1968 and 1969 a very low rate for the U.S. Employers had many job openings but were not able to find qualified employees. Yet in certain sections of the country, unemployment was very high. People wanted jobs but did not have the necessary skills. In several of our northern inner cities, the unemployment rate approached 50 percent, yet employers in these same cities could not find qualified employees to fill their job openings.

This human resource dislocation had an effect on inflation, since employers tended to bid the wage rate up for what few workers were available, and was also a contributing factor to the inner-city riots during this period since so many were without jobs in such a prosperous period of American history. The federal government reacted to this situation with several programs to hire the "hard-core unemployed" or hard-to-employ persons. The essence of these programs was to provide this advantaged group with remedial education and training, through joint federal-private business action, in the skills necessary for many entry level jobs in industry.

Even though some group have not acquired needed skills to effectively compete for jobs in a highly technological labor market, the vast majority of the U.S. labour force has acquired such skills. In fact the average formal educational level now exceeds a high school education.

The types of skills brought to the labour market by the labor force today are much more sophisticated than they were in the early 1960s. For example, various new engineering, computer, and medical technician jobs require much higher skills than previously required in these fields. Even the automotive mechanic of the 70s must be more highly skilled than his counterpart in the 60s because of the more sophisticated design of automobile engines and related auto systems, and because of the tremendous variety in automotive models within a given manufacturer's line.

Any manpower plan must assess the human resource educational/skill level of the labor market from which it draws, predict future changes in this mix, assess the effect of manpower programs, and then plan recruiting, training, and job design system that take maximum advantage of the forecasted educational/skill mix. An effective manpower plan requires a careful and accurate assessment of the present and forecasted skills of an organizations' potential employees.

Cultural values, norms, and social institutions

Many employers today are asking themselves what happened to the old - fashioned belief in hard work. This concern is but a symptom of a more general concerr many people have regarding the nature of fundamenta values which have supposedly been held by the wor force in the Indian society. Many people believe thes values are changing. Others believe that present valu are merely being redefined and arranged in a differe priority.

Perhaps societal values toward work are n changing, but norms certainly are. Values are ba beliefs which give stability to society and are slow change. Norms are guides to behaviour. They manifest represent values. Values tend to be hard to define, nor are more specific. For example, at one time the value hard work was manifested through the norm of hea physical labor. Today, hard work often means ment pressure and long hours, but not necessarily physic labour.

The conventional wisdom is that today's employee particularly younger employees, seem to want jobs tha are challenging, personally rewarding, and have opportunities for personal and professional growth. Work is not a necessary evil or something to be avoided, but rather an integral part of life, to be enjoyed to the greatest extent possible.

In addition, many people, particularly youth desire to balance the goals associated with career development with other "life-space" goals such as family life, recreation, church affairs, and civic responsibilities. Long hours of a "work-aholic" may not be personally acceptable if they interfere with goals in other areas of one's life.

These changing norms regarding work mean that organizations should examine job enrichment techniques to determine their applicability. It also means that employers should consider these changes in developing manpower plans. Today's employees expect employing organizations and other social institutions to be more responsive to the demands made upon them by the organizations' various membership groups.

Changing legal environment and manpower planning

The greatest changes in the legal environment have occurred because of legislation and executive orders instituted by the federal government. In particular, the most significant changes have been in equal employment opportunity and affirmative action, occupational safety and health, government involvement in managing the economy to minimize inflation and unemployment and maximize economic growth, and more comprehensive coverage of wage and hour legislation.

At the state level, laws have been passed by many states to legalize collective bargaining in public employment. This means that unions and collective bargaining procedures are becoming increasingly more common in state, city, and county units.

These changes in the legal environment are an extension of a trend begun in the 1930s to give employees more rights, and hence more power, in dealing with employers. From the Federal Wage and Hour law and the Wagner Act, which legalized unions in the private sector in the thirties, to Title VII of the 1964 Civil Rights Act, and the 1970 Occupational Safety and Health Act, employer action toward employees has become increasingly more constrained. No longer can an employer hire only white males, pay them what he wishes, and work them in an unsafe environment. He must now abide by equal employment regulations, pay at least the minimum wage and time and one-half for overtime, and meet the minimum safety requirements in his operations as specified by the Occupational Safety and Health Act.

Why has such legislation been passed to regulate employer treatment of employees? The primary reason is because the operation of the labour market did not regulate such behavior. The economic power of todays' large employers in the labor market would far exceed the power of the individual worker in the absence of protective legislation. If the marked did effectively regulate these practices, how could we have ever had women and children working twelve to fourteen hours per day seven days a week for a subsistence wage under sweat-shop conditions? These conditions were all too common at the turn of the century in our factories.

The role of government is to pass laws to achieve the public good. When the public good outweights private property rights, government will pass laws to constrain these rights. Witness zoning laws, laws against prostitution and drugs, anti-monopoly laws as well as federal and state regulation of various industries such as airlines, railroads, transmission lines, utilities, and communications. In each case, it is believed that the public good would not be served in the absence of such regulations.

The same argument holds with legislation which affects the employer-employee relationship. The effect of the changing legal environment has been to improve wages, working conditions, and terms and conditions of employment for the average employee, thus leading to the accomplishment of the public good. Employer manpower plans have changed over time to be in conformity with the legislation and will continue to change as additional legislation is passed.

Designing a human resource information system-manpower planning in the firm

Our discussion thus far has been concerned with the macro aspects of manpower planning. Macro manpower planning sets the environment for micro manpower planning in the organization. The objective of the internal manpower planning process for an organization is to insure that adequate manpower with the desired skills and abilities are available when and where they are needed.

The manpower planning process is a major component of an organization's *human resource information system.* The concept of the human resource information system developed as a result of the work by Likert, Brummet, Pyle, Flamholtz, and others at the University of Michigan in the late 1960s. A major portion of a human resource information system is the system of human resource accounting. *Human Resource Accounting* is an attempt to assign a Rs. value to an organization's human resources. Such components as the amounts an organization has invested in its human resources through training and development, hiring and replacement costs, employee salaries, and turnover costs are usually used to computer the worth of an organization's human resources.

Human resource accounting systems today have evolved to the point of "identifying, measuring, and communicating information about human resources in order to facilitate effective management within an organization. Management requires information regarding resource acquisition, development, maintenance, and utilization.

Thus, today's human resource accounting system is in actuality a part of the total human resource information system. Not only are the human resources assigned a value for accounting purposes, but other information concerning human resource is gathered, coded, analyzed, stored, and disseminated to managers. This information includes the following components:

1. Demographic information: age, sex, race, educational levels, marital status.
2. Skills and abilities
3. Aspiration levels
4. Performance appraisals
5. Company sponsored training programs or other training and education completed since employed.
6. Past work assignments and job title before and since being hired
7. Special notations

Most organizations gather some or even all of these informational components, but few have developed a total information system that updates this information and makes it available to appropriate managers in a comprehensive fashion. Simply relying on the traditional personnel records system for gathering, analyzing, storing, and distributing information on an organizations' human resources will not produce the quality and quantity of human resource information needed for a comprehensive manpower plan.

Constructing manpower plan

The first step in constructing a manpower plan is to determine the organization's growth and market objectives. These objectives serve as the foundation for estimating the forecasted demand for human resources in the organization. These objectives may be expressed in terms of sales, market share, return on investment, development of new products and services, and development of new markets. These objectives ought to be expressed in terms of some time frame of *planning horizon*- the length of time over which the objectives and the plan for accomplishing them will occur.

The planning horizon for many organizations seldom exceeds fifteen year and is often expressed in terms of short-range, intermediate-range, and long-range periods. As a rule of thumb, short-ranges is a horizon of one year or less, intermediate-range of two to six years, and long-range of seven to fifteen years. Often the long-range objectives are quite general, and the intermediate and short-range objectives much more specific. This specificity is especially true of short-range or *operational* objectives.

Procedures for specifying objectives and the means for their accomplishment generally fall under the heading of *Management by Objectives* in the management literature. The determination of sound, long-range, intermediate-range, short-range organizational and associated departmental objectives is essential for an effective manpower plan, and the management by objectives technique is very effective for developing and specifying objectives.

Once the organization's objectives are specified, communicated and understood by all affected, then the personnel or manpower planning unit should specify their objectives with regard to human resource utilization in the organization. In developing these objectives, specific policies need to be formulated which address the following questions:

1. Shall we attempt to fill positions from within or by hiring individuals from the labor market? More specifically:
   a. What we do hope to accomplish from promotion from within and why?
   b. What jobs shall we fill by promotion?
   c. Does our organization have the needed skills and, if not, can our people be trained and developed for these jobs?
   d. What types of skills exist in our relevant labor market, and can we effectively recruit and attract people from this market?
   e. What effect will bringing in people from the outside have on our presently employed people?
2. Can we meet our commitments to affirmative action and equal employment opportunity?
3. How do our training and development objectives interface with our manpower planning objectives?
4. What union constraints do we face in manpower planning, and what policies should we develop to effectively handle these constraints?
5. What is our policy toward providing everyone in the organization with a meaningful, challenging job? Will we continue to have some boring, routine jobs or should we be eliminating them?

The third step in the process is to estimate the skills and number of people required for the organization by occupational category for the planning horizon. Occupational skills change over time.

Therefore, it is important at this stage that an organization have a complete, current listing of all occupational categories in the organization with explanatory job description which specify the duties, skills, and qualifications required for each job. It should also attempt to forecast future changes in the duties, skills, and qualifications for these positions based on changes in technological requirements and the aspiration levels of individuals in the organization and the external labour market.

Fourth, the planner should estimate the manpower shortage or surplus for each occupational and job category and should determine what it plans to do about any estimated surplus or shortage in view of the human resource utilization objectives.

Note that this procedure ties in consideration of human resources objectives in filling jobs from within via internal promotions and organizational growth objectives.

If a surplus is predicted for an occupational category, the human resources planner needs to determine if these individuals will be discharged, temporarily laid off, transferred without any training, provided with training and then transferred, or provided with a cash bonus for quitting. These decisions will probably by determined by the organizations' overall human resource objectives for training and development.

If a shortage is predicted, then the organization must resort to the external labor market if it expects to fill the resulting job vacancies. This decision may cause the organization to review its human resource objectives with regard to hiring in the external market vis-a-vis other objectives. The final step is to establish specific recruiting, selection, placement, training, compensation, and promotion objectives, plans, and policies to meet the estimated vacancies.

3

Manpower Development and Organisation Development

It can be claimed that the most effective manpower development can only be achieved if the two functions work in close collaboration, and if at the same time general management are fully aware of the overlapping interests, and the interactions, of the two. It is recognised by those who actually watch organisations at work-as distinct from writing or reading books on organisation-that, whatever the formal nature of an organisation, as reflected in the organisaton charts, the job descriptions and accountability statements, the way it works is dependent on the capabilities, relationship and agreements amongst the people within the organisation. Sometimes these interpersonal relationships are in conflict with the written organisation definitions cannot think of everything.

It is also recognised that the people within the organisation must have freedom to adapt and change, according to their strengths and weaknesses, preferences and dislikes, if that organisation is to keep going in the constantly changing human and economic world in which the company operates. Rigidity beyond a certain point is not desirable if managers and executives are expected to respond rapidly to changes in their workloads and problems. Our interest at this moment is to see the way in which organisaton and changes in organisation, formal or informal, effect the manpower development work which is being carried out within that organisation.

A common impact of manpower development on organisation arises from the deliberate provision of places for trainees. The apprentice requiring real shop floor experience, the graduate who needs to gain wide experience with minimum delay, the supervisors designate who require exposure to apposite aspects of company work, the thin stream of high flyers who must build up expertise faster than anyone else; all of these people may only get what they require in the way or work experience by a special provision. If they all have to wait in the queue all of the time, the training and development may be impossible to achieve. Some will be possible through normal internal posting and transfer mechanisms, but not all. Indeed, it may be seen as undesirable to maximise the movement of trainees through the normal internal cogency opportunities, for this might block many opportunities for those who were members of development schemes but who nevertheless merited a transfer or a promotion.

So some posts or workplaces may have to be created or isolated for development purposes; and this has an effect on organisation structures and the distribution of responsibility. The first effect is the likely increase in the numbers of people in the particular work area, although this need not always be the case when introducing trainees of high calibre. The second effect may then be to create increased supervision, because there are now more employees and the additional ones have an exceptional need for being taught. This is common within apprenticeship schemes. The older and the more sophisticated the learner, the less inclined management are to create new workplaces, and the less inclined are the people already in that work area to accept a stranger in their midst, a stranger who is there to advance his own career at, they may believe, their expense in time and effort.

If the trainees thus posted are good and hard working, and, above all, interested in what they are given to do, they might be quickly assimilated. They may even become indispensable; and this can lead to problems of manpower growth if a strict watch is not kept on the nature of the work undertaken by both trainees and regular employees. A popular trainee group may even create a subtle expansion pressure in the company, should line and manpower managers both prefer to take into their growing establishments such people, beyond their real needs, but too good to let go elsewhere. Jumping to the other end of the scale we find, for example, the creation of understudy posts at high levels in the hierarchy, in order to provide an insight into more rarified aspects of management for one person, or for a procession of people. Understudy posts can be most successful, it is generally found, if the bulk of the work to be done by the understudy is real and responsible work. Otherwise he is unable to penetrate into the problems and the minds of people around him. If the understudy is given real work to do, where does it come from? From the boss's workload, or from people around him in the organisation? Will the incumbent then inflate the importance of his work until the work becomes recognised as being necessary to the area in which he is working, and so critical that it can never be handed back to those who lent it to him in the first place? Such things do happen. The company may now find itself not only with an extra permanent post, but also with a new division of responsibilities between a group of managers or supervisors in that part of the organisation.

Although these problems may rarely be serious in well established companies in the West, their importance is much greater in companies starting up with inexperienced local labour, or undergoing rapid localisation and growth, in the developing countries. In these cases it would be often unrealistic initially to create hierarchies, structure and job responsibilities based on the Western patterns, although the temptation to do so is extremely great.

The existing levels of knowledge and experiences are relatively low, and therefore the capital potential and ready adaptation of people into new work somewhat unreliable. The capability of anyone to teach his colleagues or his juniors much may be also low and therefore organisation and relationships must be developed in some way that will enhance to a maximum the learning opportunities. These should include heuristic principles if this learning and the accompanying interest growth is to be made the most of. Deterministic planning, and manpower development to suit, is most effective where there is high confidence, with evidence to support that confidence; and such planning demands reasonably well worked out structures through which those chosen can worked their way.

Thus organisation development and manpower development must, in these grass roots circumstances, go hand in hand. The work for any individual must not greatly exceed his initial capability, yet it must provide room for 'stretching' and the development on new interest. This may mean that there have to be six in a work unit where otherwise four would be sufficient. But if there are six, with the need for even more supervision than otherwise, attention needs to be paid to the number of supervisors needed, and the levels and sorts of responsibility they are to carry. Clearly their training and development responsibility could be greater than in other older and more experienced companies. With the increase in numbers of supervisory roles at the lower edge of the company, there is an increased pressure on promotion vacancies a little higher up. Does this mean an automatic increase in the number of posts at that higher level? Maybe this is in any case desirable because of the problems for the inexperienced in handling the management workload. Thus one can see a total inflation, vitally necessary perhaps, throughout the company. This increases the fragmentation and decreases the spontaneous communication in the company, both of which are counter-productive and it adds, of course, to the normal manpower control problems of wastage and replacement.

In companies like this, in which a great deal of teaching, learning and personal development is taking place, it is usual to expect to find not only the growth of personal ambition, but also the assumption of a great deal of personal expectation. Socioeconomic studies show how expectation provides incentive to action for some, and a mere demand for satisfaction for others. When the growth rate in the standard of living in any country slows up then dissatisfaction will be felt and expressed, even though there may be no actual decline in the absolute standard of living. Similarly in companies; if the rate of advancement of employees slows up noticeably as the company reaches the end of a growth and promotion phase of localisation there will be a sense of disappointment universally felt amongst the employees.

This disappointment will occur at a time when there is every reason to maintain the stimuli of training and other educational processes, for heuristic and work-day purposes; and this may produce in turn a sourness amongst the employees who associated training and education with pretty rapid promotion and salary advancement, which is now on the wane. This now gives organisation development a new objective. Previously it had been concerned with the structures of a company in which the growth rate will be much smaller, where ambition may have turned to cynicism, but even so where the continued development of management, executive, and all other individual capability is vital.

We must add two further causes of problem to the above. Localisation, in developing countries in particular, can run into age-structure problems from the outset. It is not unusual to find there that much of the educational development in the country is recent. Hence the cadre of people in the company who are regard as being of high technical potential, all fall within a relatively narrow age band, and are probably relatively young. Moreover, those who are the youngest in this group may be the best educated of them all, as a result of the development of educational policies over a period of as little as ten or 15 years.

It would not be surprising to find therefore that there are middle managers in their early thirties, well qualified and trained, who realistically regard their chances of promotion in the foreseeable future as very slight; they know that the ages of those above them are mainly in the middle and late thirties bracket. There must be a very long time to wait before stepping into anyone's shoes unless special measures are taken. Not only has the organisational growth slowed right down, but in addition the natural manpower upward flow rate will in itself be very slow.

This type of problem is met anywhere in the world, and it has become recognised as one which normally needs attention if the resulting stagnation is to be avoided. For the stagnation can produce not merely frustration for the ambitious, but a staleness and loss or creativity and flexibility even in those who are content to accept their lot. At this point organisation development may well become almost indistinguishable from manpower development, for the main question to be dealt with is how to produce structures which provide career satisfaction and progressive work whilst at the same time meet the functional need of the company.

There is a limit to the number of artificial organisation changes that can be effectively made with this short of objective in mind. Some changes may be accompanied by a loss of self respect but this depends on the sensitivity of the person then moved or promoted; and there is a loss in working efficiency in areas where one or more of the appointments inactually unnecessary. But fortunately where are other factors at work which can relieve the pressures inside the company. These we shall consider briefly.

Companies which approach their manpower development in a conscientious way may become over-possessive about the people who work in the company, and may regard the loss of people to the outside world as a sort of failure. But however one regards losses, they inevitably happen, and are part of the manpower equations of the company. Losses in personnel, occurring at the right levels of employment, can actually be an advantage to the company. It would relieve the pressure on management to invent organisational ways of sustaining the motivation of junior and middle executive levels if there were sufficient losses in the middle and senior groups. There can be no question of the company's being unconcerned as to how many, and which, people leave; but there is a definite advantage to be considered as arising from losses uncertain instances.

Fortunately the economic situation which gives rise to the sudden and accelerated growth of a company, may create a demand for skilled and experienced people in the outside labour market. If this is the case then the losses, to other companies, to the government, to education, can be as an advantage to the company in overall terms, and might be encouraged through frank disclosure of the limitations to career and personal development in the company, as it is presently manned.

If, however, the company itself envisages a future growth in its own activities then it may able to use the future growth as a proper means of absorbing that excess fraction of its manpower which, apart from being an extra expense, is impeding its efficiency at present.

The right organisation

We have considered above how the provision of jobs for training and development purpose affects the size, the structure and some of the job responsibilities of a company, and how in the extreme a company's structures may be dominated by factors arising from the need to devote so much effort to the employment and development of people of whom a large proportion have an outstanding learning need. We should look now at the question of what sort of organisation is required to best accommodate people who have learned what they have been set to learn, and are no longer considered as predominantly learners, but as doers, as executives or managers.

This may not seem to be an important question to those who believe that an organisation is created by drawing a chart showing the various hierarchical levels, defining the responsibilities of and relationship between all jobs, and then posting people, suitably chosen, into all the positions in the hierarchy. At any time when the operations of the operations of the company change, that organisation can be changed in all appropriate details, and those affected can be rebriefed and retrained if necessary. This is the classic drawing board approach that is compatible with the deterministic principle of manpower development, but it is not so compatible with the use of the heuristic principle. We have seen that it is likely that the use of the three principles of development follows the following pattern. For the most junior and elementary trainee and development purposes, heuristic principles may be often used. For middle and junior levels there will less use of heuristic principles and more dependence on a probabilistic approach coupled with a short term deterministic final decision for each ultimate appointment. At the top levels the deterministic approach will predominate. We have seen, however, that wherever heuristics can be used then the interest, energy and capability levels of those involved are likely to be higher than otherwise.

We have been using the word heuristic to apply to learning method. The principle can be extended, and this was referred to earlier, to include the ultimate selection by the person concerned (the learner) of what he is to do. We have seen that some companies attempt to introduce this element of choice into the career development of employees. What is possible, in addition to the normal use of heuristics for individual learning, is its extension into organisation development. One is getting close to this in the exploratory discovery and learning by the individual, when that discovery and learning is about relationship with other people and other functions in his work area. If the other people at the same time are able to examine these same relationships, then, given senior management agreement, there may be an organisational change or development, albeit a small one.

If this is extend further across the organisaton then we would produce organisational development based on the heuristic learning and adaptations of people across the whole network of the organisation. This is familiar concept enough to the OD specialist, who would be interested also in ensuring that the small changes adaptations and development added up to somethin that was of advantage to the whole organisaton. There are ways of dealing with this, based on providing information that will enable each person to see and understand the whole situation of which he is a part.

What is of significance to organisational development is that the more the company pursues the heuristic principle for its training more the company pursues the heuristic principle for its training and development, the more likely it is that those who benefit by this may spontaneously employ it in a search for improvements in organisation. The new forms of organisation will reflect, and use, individual capabilities, with a commensurate release of energy and dedication, instead of persuading or forcing people to adapt into roles created by third party decisions.

4

Manpower Planning and its Development

People grow in number of ways. Their Level of knowledge develops through a variety of learning situations, ranging from reading or watching, and various forms of education and training, to work experience doing a permanent job or part-or full-time assignments or projects. In addition to the acquisition of knowledge, some of these activities build self-confidence and competence, and encourage the development of personality, visible through improved social skills. The ability to make good decisions based on inadequate information while under pressure may be one of the abilities which a young manager develops from an operational assignment. Only by doing can be get a real appreciation of the demands and complexity of higher level work.

People develop far more from doing, from exposure and response to changing opportunities, than by any other means, although the use of training to supplement experience and prepare for further assignments is also important. A planned sequence of jobs, selected to fit developing abilities and personal preferences, and preferably under development-conscious managers, will produce the fastest growth towards ultimate potential.

The process of personal development should designed to maximize the pace of relevant learning and personal growth by planning appropriate deployments, identifying the stage at which learning opportunities will be exhausted, and acknowledging the need to initiate fresh assignments to maintain intellectual stimulate.

The designing and planning of development must be emphasized, for it rarely happens casually. Development assignments have been likened to moving plants from the greenhouse to the garden. The ground needs to be prepared and the seedlings must be brought to readiness; then they will need some protection, particularly in the early stages, and need to be watched initially in case they become battered by the environment. It is the development opportunity, far more than anything else, which enables people to grow.

The elements of development

There are numerous actions or elements in an individual development plan, including:

- Planned work experience, which should be challenging and followed by reassignment when learning opportunities in a job are exhausted, and project work and secondments, either internal or external, full-or part-time.
- Training, to provide the knowledge and skills required in current and possible future jobs, and to bring technical knowledge up to date.
- Further education towards professional qualifications, or to develop language skills, etc. Also, other self-learning and professional reading.
- Coaching, mentoring and counselling.

Most of this list is straightforward, but it is worth commenting that multifunctional project teams provide particularly good developmental experience of other functions and of the working of the business.

Mentors

To facilitate optimum growth, the use of a high level tutor to oversee the progress of each high potential individual, to talk with him periodically and influence the direction of his development, can be invaluable and should be encouraged. The mentor can stimulate and guide the developing individual, and also irritate the company to ensure timely action is taken to prepare the next deployment or relevant training of his charge. With more time to devote to development issues than a direct line boss, and more clout than an adviser from human resources, the mentor can more effectively ensure that the right things are done. In this respect, they provide invaluable support.

In addition to mentors, some direct line managers are exceptionally effective as developers and motivators of their subordinates. These managers need to be identified and utilized as a critically important resource. They deserve to be allocated the best candidates for they are likely to guide the growth of these people through any difficulties and to produce the best development subordinates.

Development jobs

One of the best ways of developing experience is by assignment to carefully jobs. Many companies believe that some jobs are especially valuable for this purpose, and designate them as development jobs. These are reserved exclusively for the higher ability young managers as definitive steps in their personal growth. Such posts include, for example, the general managership of smaller businesses where an individual can get to grips with a full business for the first time and take responsibility for profits.

In practice, we find that development requirements are so diverse that only a small proportion of needs are adequately met by the designated development slots. Only when the total range of jobs is covered in developmental assignments can needs be met fully.

A simple exchange of positions for a set period can be valuable. It allows a manager who is progressing slowly to be returned to his old post after a two year stint elsewhere, while the faster moving manager is assigned to his next career challenge. Alternatively, the manager whose position is borrowed may undertake a project assignment for his own further development.

Although it is advisable not to shuffle managers too frequently, it is equally as important to make sure that no-one stagnates. Development planning should create real pressure for change whenever this appears to be happening.

Individual development plans

A management development system needs to cover every individual with any real potential for personal development. An individual development plan (IDP) should exist, however simple in format, for all of these people, from graduate intake level up to, and including, board members. Based on all available objective information about each individual plus future organization and management requirement data, the IDP should record how we expect the individual to develop over the next several years, including alternative options where appropriate, and detail development plans, training requirements and anticipated appointments.

These are working documents, continually added to and annotated as plans or moves are auctioned, and monitored to ensure plans are implemented. They sit with the line manager as a reminder of his commitment to planned actions, but management development staff should monitor progress. The quality of the evaluation is critically important to the future, both for the individuals and for the company, because it allows any limitations in the process to be identified and corrected.

Ready to move

Within the development process, it is vital to identify those individuals who are ready for fresh assignments and further stretching so that action to move them on to their next assignments can be taken early. Their further growth is essential and must be followed through, however valuable they may be in their present roles. To slow or block the growth of an individual is likely to lead to him leaving the company.

Periodic reviews of the abilities and readiness to move of all career staff are essential, and every vacancy provides a development opportunity. Ideal next assignments should be determined, together with provisional timing, so that moves can be planned ahead to ensure continuity. Where no local opportunity exists able individual who is becoming ready for a move, wider opportunities should be each individual should be evident on his IDP and is part of the overall management inventory.

Individual development plan content

An IDP is a brief summary of key information related to the individual's forward career plan. The form of an IDP can vary enormously, from blank sheets to complex forms. However, it is likely to contain;

Identification:	Name
	Job title, company, location, grade.
	Date of birth/age.
Summary of career/	Qualifications/major training courses

experience:	attended. Dates/companies/positions/major achievements.
Strengths:	Summary of major strengths relevant to future job possibilities.
Limitations:	Notes on any factors which may restrict the scope or direction of his future development, or which need to be overcome by experience or training.
Personal preferences:	Mobility. Job type. Extent of ambition.
Development action plans:	
Job:	Ready for move, when? Next job/options/timing. Specific appointment planned.
Other factors:	Training plans to meet agreed needs. Actions to overcome critical limitations. Experience needs to be met.

Preparing an IDP is the easy part. It is implementation which causes the headaches. As with any other plan, it represents the best effort at the time the plan is made, but the business situation and environment change endlessly, as do the pace of individual development, personal preferences and mobility, and the availability of opportunities, so reviews must take place regularly.

Any plan needs to be kept close at hand so that progress can be monitored. Concern only arises when the plans agreed in an managers should audit the progress of development plans within their own area, with some overview by the next managerial level. There should be should business justification for changes, and evidence that the plan has been rethought and individual actions reschedules. If this is not happening, it may be legitimate to ask why expensive management time is being wasted developing plans it is not intending to implement.

Career paths

For many lower level jobs, training and preparation are targeted on one job or a limited range of options, with little expectation that the great majority of incumbents will show any potential for further advancement. A small number will progress into supervisory posts, largely in the area, and a few may show some ability to progress in other ways.

It is in the area of professional and managerial staff that career paths with organized flows are relevant. Career paths are designed to encourage systematic development of numbers of similar individuals, such as the graduate or professional staff intake, to ensure that each has the opportunity to participate in the full range of training and to gain experience in a planned range of relevant activities, and then to progress logically along the most suitable career development route.

These routes can be relatively simple for most people, for the bulk of the further manager intake will enter through a chosen function, and concentrate initially on developing their knowledge and skills within that chosen area. Most will seek a variety of experience to cover all aspects of that function before concentrating on more specific operating roles within it, or a specialist aspect.

The bulk of career progression probably takes place within single functions, with only a relatively small proportion of people deliberately or casually moving between career streams. The company is likely to want a small core of high ability people to gain multi-functional experience as a foundation to general management or to top functional posts, but it would see little advantage from more widespread interchange. Similarly, for employees generally, their market values represent the sum of their knowledge and experience, and their ability to apply it, so any move to a fresh function not subsidized by management would involve a drop in value and this is rarely acceptable.

If early development is within one function, it is logical to define stages and to encourage some systematic progression through them. Normal rates of flow should evolve so that requirements could be forecast, and the core training relevant to each stage should be clear. However, the rate of individual progress should vary with performance, and appraisals will show how quickly an individual gets on top of the demands at each level, and assessments of potential show ability to cope with higher and wider ranging assignments.

Where career development expands to include more than one career path, the pattern may develop with crisscrossing between the line and functional roles within one function, or between primary functions and assignments in other major functions, or by progressive appointments alternating between general and functional management.

There must be purpose behind individual can progressions of this type. The longer term intention might involve developing a high ability individual towards a much more senior post, with a series of hurdles to be overcome in the process. Such a career path has a distinctly higher than normal level of risk, although it may have a similarly high level of potential reward. The responsibility for the risk element should be accepted by the company in that it is the company that is taking the critical decisions to appoint the individual and it will have assessed the form and extent of the risk in advance and judged that it can be overcome. If there is a failure, and there will be some, it must be handled sympathetically as a learning experience, so that career damage is minimized for the individual, who continues to be a valuable corporate resource. Indeed, the reason for failure may be an unexpected change in the business environment which an inexperienced man could not be expected to handle.

Future organizations appear to require greater degrees of specialization, combined with a wider appreciation of where each function's contribution fits into the overall business, plus an understanding of the overall business operation. This will develop in part by the increasing use of project teams, which provide extensive cross-functional experience, and also through management training modules designed to set individual specialist areas in the context of the broader business.

Self-Development

Most employees are acutely interested and active in progressing their own development. The days are long gone when an individual accepted that his development and career would be taken care of by the company and the he would do the jobs to which he was assigned and go where he was sent. Today, individuals not only expect to be involved in the direction of their career development, but are likely to express strong views on their preferences and take initiatives to achieve their career objectives. Ideally, development becomes a partnership, with the company pursuing its needs in open discussion with its staff.

Self-awareness

Self-development is logically proceeded by self-awarenes. Some organizations now run short seminars or development centres for groups of bright younger managers, which are designed to increase self-knowledge or self-awareness and to help clarify the soundness and achievability of personal career objectives and development plans.

These sessions draw out information on a range of aspects. They provide insights into personality and how other people see the individual. For example, a degree of introversion and poor relationship building might be highlighted, which may not have been understood previously and can restrict career development. The process should also explore how individuals learn and their style of learning, and may explore and challenge the personal philosophies of the participants.

Career development options

It is unlikely that the forward view will take the form of a clear single career line. Invariable there will be options but, to some extent, the options which are taken will be heavily influenced by the timing of opportunities becoming available. The chance to take to promotion is difficult to turn down if the preferred alternative is less immediate and less certain.

The task facing each individual is to identify a range if options which seem achievable from the starting point, and then to add some desirable but less realistic possibilities, with notes of the actions which would be required to make them achievable. For example, the individual trained as an accountant is likely to identify a range of straightforward options associated with progression from his initial functional training, but if he wants to progress to general management, there will be range of additional criteria to meet.

Each individual needs to assess the options available from where he is now, weighed against his preferences, ambitions, mobility and what he seeks from life, and then determine the strength of preference for a particular track.

Career development is a partnership owned, jointly by the manager and his manager, but in which neither has total freedom of action and each has different objectives. The boss knows that he must plan to meet the manpower needs of his organization, based on business objectives and environment. In parallel, he will want to deploy his manpower inventory as efficiently as possible while optimizing development opportunities for all individuals, some of whom may have career objectives not available within the company.

Managers who develop subordinates well

In every organization there are some managers who seem to have a golden touch with the development of their subordinates. People in their areas are encouraged and guided to develop rapidly and, subsequently, feature strongly in the lists of promoted individuals. In contrast, there are other manager who appear to place a dead hand on the careers of their subordinates. Inevitably, there is competition amongst the better younger managers to join one of the forcing houses, and great to avoid getting trapped in a dead end.

Observations of the development environment enable an individual to decide whether the company will be supportive in helping him to develop his career along the line he had in mind. However, while this support is invaluable, the main drive and effort must come from himself.

Preferences, ambitions and mobility

Career development is strongly related to abilities but

individual preferences, ambitions and mobility have a substantial influence and are liable to change. Knowledge of these influences is an essential ingredient in assembling and agreeing realistic development plans which set out the intended or most likely career paths for individuals.

There is a joint responsibility on the part of manager and subordinate to ensure that the company has sufficient awareness of each employee's view of his future, which should be on the agenda at most counselling sessions.

During the early years of career development, there are generally several avenues open for the next move and many individuals have clear preferences which influence the vacancies they choose to go after. One key consideration will be around the degree of specialization preferred. Those who aspire to top management may seek to broaden their experience through a number of diverse assignments to develop a generalist C.V., while other may find their career satisfaction comes from growing in a specialist function.

Selection of preferred activities may be influence by ultimate career ambition, but other factors are present. Preferred life-style is increasingly influencing willingness to work in some of the more demanding workaholic organizations which attract some individuals who are willing to make such a commitment, but repel others. In this way, the culture of an organization, as perceived from outside, has a significant impact on employment image and its ability to attract able candidates from outside.

We have to learn to live with the view and career preferences of our people, but if we believe that the capabilities an individual fall short of his ambitions, the disagreement may be serious. Participation in a self-awareness seminar with strong feedback from a group of peers my lead an individual to reassess his objectives and achieve greater realism.

When the opportunity arises an attractive appointment involving a significant geographic move, at least one third of the immediate acceptances seem to get reversed after the partner or family become involved. In most of those cases, the partner may have given a casual agreement to the concept of mobility, but react differently when faced with a reality. For the planning of potential overseas postings, the discussion has to be blunt and specific from an early stage to ensure commitment.

Career progression in some large organizations has been linked traditionally to mobility. Development required that an individual did not spend too long in one place, and was rarely promoted without a transfer. The banks and the church were good examples; large multinationals provide another. This policy is changing, and large organizations appear to be seeking new and acceptable rules. Acceptability is recognized because individual attitudes to mobility are far less permissive than a couple of decades back. Company attitudes have been influenced also by the high costs of transfers and the difficulties arising from enormous regional variations in house prices. Associated flow patterns need monitoring.

Career mobility is still expected from high ability, intensely ambitious individuals, who are clearly heading for high positions where some variation in experience and working environments is seen as essential. These committed individuals are likely to accept the opportunities to advance which are offered, and the employer is likely to have strong views on the experience it requires in its top people. The cost factor is irrelevant where the number of people is small and their future vital to the organization.

Mobility seems particularly relevant in large multinationals where those individuals who aspire to senior positions will find themselves managing and doing business across cultural boundaries. It is essential for these people to gain first-hand experience in more than one situation. In these companies, the evolving pattern requires the high performing stream to undertake foreign assignments from an early state, in the knowledge that there are career bars for those who lack international experience.

People following functional careers in categories where organizations employ relatively small numbers also need to be mobile to progress. These may be only limited opportunity for internal career advancement, so individuals are faced with developing their careers by changing employment or accepting slower advancement as they wait for convenient opportunities to arise. Career planning is likely to assume and encourage mobility within the function and across the corporation, so knowledge of the real extent of individual mobility is important.

Development of high potential

The most important resource in the care of any board of directors is the select cadre of high potential younger mangers, which will provide the primary source of candidates for senior management and board positions in ten to 20 years' time. The career development of this elite group is increasing under the hand of the CEO personally.

There is a great deal of difference between our view of the potential of a newly recruited graduate and our view of further potential in an established senior manager. Although significant potential can exist at all levels and age should not be a bar, younger managers do learn and develop fastest.

Mid-20s Up through the mid-20s, there is not likely to be any substantial track record to demonstrate evidence of potential, Judgements made will be based on intellectual strength, personality and perhaps the degree of maturity evident. The first years of post-academic achievements are visible, indicating the ability to adapt to a fresh situation and make things happen. The embrionic track record is likely to look good and early career plans have begun to test and stretch capability. This has been described as the exploratory stage of a career. At this age, the apparent fliers tend to be those who appear more mature, are always quite certain of what they are going to do, aware working hard to get there.

Age 28-32 This period seems to provide the critical decision taking stage in which most employers assess potential. It is at this point that track records seem to be showing clear indications about which individuals learn fast, cope with new situations, and show a grasp of broader business essentials. All of the available information is assembled to determine what is really indicated about future potential as distinct from past performance. The quality of career plans to test and stretch abilities now shows through, for those considered to have above average potential should have been place in appointments and assignments which tested capabilities beyond their present levels.

At this stage, many companies supplement their data by making use of assessment centres which provide more detailed information on the extent and form of potential, and talk out detailed IDPs which take into account apparent potential, individual preferences, and future opportunities.

The 30s These years provide a period of great testing and stretching as individuals climb their chosen paths at varying speeds. Some will continue to show an astonishing ability to grasp the complexities of new situations quickly and make real contributions while, for others, the pace is simply slower, or a ceiling is reached.

The 40s In the 40s, the high potential stream has thinned out considerably, and now contains only the small number of highly placed individuals who are thought to retain the potential for significant further advance. The testing and evaluation of this group to determine their suitability for the highest offices will be ongoing.

There are many individuals who will be assessed as having potential for further advancement well beyond their 40s and no cut-off point is implied here. In fact, most managers have some further potential at all stages of their careers, but high potential implies the ability to achieve significant further advance in a short period of time, and that does become progressively more rare.

Organizations which actively manage the process of development gain a significant competitive advantage. Research in the US has shown a correlation between success in top management and the breadth of experience, showing that slightly less successful top managers in the same enterprise had rather less breadth experience.

Test and stretch

One problem in managing development effectively is that the timing of readiness for advancement is most difficult to predict. The individuals' proven abilities and their needs must be comprehensively understood, and assignments found for them in which they are challenged to the limit and must strive hard to cope. That can be a critical time if any unexpected development occurs, but the next level of management should be on the alert to provide support if necessary. In the process these individuals grow rapidly, but all too quickly they complete or get on top of the task and, once again, begin to show readiness for the next. It is, of course, essential that the next challenge be provided, even if this means giving priority to young high potential managers when more proven ability is available.

Inevitably, not every challenge is tackled smoothly. There can be errors of assignment, or the business may conspire to produce an unplanned set of environmental changes. If failure occurs, there must be commitment to support any individual placed in a test and stretch position. If blame must be allocated for a failure, it falls largely on those who approved the appointment. The main objective in such a situation must be to recover the confidence and upward movement of the candidate by placing him or her quickly in a fresh assignment with a high probability of success, and not recording a black mark. As one CEO noted: 'When they stumble, they should be counselled in a way that shows them how to succeed rather than be shoved off the list of hot prospects.'

People management skills

One group of skills more than any other is gaining importance as a critical characteristic of future senior managers. The role of a manager involves getting things done through other people. He is responsible for some of these people whereas others will be his equals or superiors, or his customers and suppliers. His effectiveness as a manager and his ultimate performance will depend on personal relationships and his ability to get things done. As each manger exist within an enterprise, the task is to manage through the system and structure; to get things done through people within the organization, systems and cultures in which they all exist.

In observing subordinate managers of high potential, the way in which they mange their staff (and other personal relationships) should be watched closely to see whether staff follow their leadership. They should be seen to encourage open communication, be sensitive to others and handle people firmly yet compassionately, handle older subordinates well and gain their respect, and develop their subordinates. If these things are going well, it provides another positive element in the growing track record.

Monitor progress

Feedback of progress on development assignments should be recorded on IDPs so that a comprehensive track record accumulates. If career limiting factors are identified, they must be recorded and action planned to overcome them if possible. They do not disappear if they are ignored and are liable to occur more severely and cause career difficulties if not tackled. Some may limit career prospects, but identification should restrict damage and ensure that evident potential is directed to a career not threatened by the limitation.

The optimum career path for a high potential candidate should be outlined for a five-to 10-year period, with ideal postings noted and selected to provide the mix of experience sought. If one of those positions is filled by a long-term incumbent, and it is considered essential to provide experience in that specific slot, then priority may need to be given to the longer term development of the high potential candidate and a fresh assignment found for the blocking individual. If this seems ruthless, one might also consider the positive aspects of a fresh assignment for a manager who has been stuck, possibly for too long, in a previous position.

Ultimately, further progress becomes more competitive as the numbers of jobs at each level decreases. Even when people reach board level it remains essential to seek indicators of further potential, and continuing growth towards the highest position should be encouraged and tested. The human resource area is an excellent example of where this should occur; senior specialists have the expertise and the time to influence behaviour and systems, and to make things happen. Much of what is in this book makes complete sense to line mangers but also presents then with problems of implementation. It is for the business planning and human resource specialists to quietly guide and assist their collegues in achieving the desired end results.

Increasing specialization is one of the major themes to emerge from predicted future organizations. Hence, specialists are likely to become a more significant element in the organization structures and manpower plans which develop through the 1990s. Specialists will find strong roles in the project management culture, where roles and objectives will be clear and require minimal supervision.

Career development for specialists will change from rather than become more limited. They will be able to move up within their own specialism, but movement specialism will be difficult or impossible. They will have great awareness of other specialism through working in task forces, but few will become true generalists. Generalists are likely to evolve from task force leaders, although leadership will be informal as specialists work together in task forces on equal terms. Compensation potential will be as great for specialists as for generalists. Large consulting and law practices provide parallels already.

5

Manpower Planning and Training Needs

Development is about total growth of the knowledge, experience and abilities of an individual, the development of the whole person as he progresses towards his ultimate potential. Development is long term and future orientated; it provides new perspectives and encourages strategic vision. In contrast, training tends to be narrower and shorter term, and is concerned with helping people to do their jobs better or preparing them for future positions. Training is one part of the development process, to which it contributes by providing supplementary opportunities to acquire knowledge, skills and attitudes largely off-the-job and to help achieve desired performance levels.

A broad business justification for training might be that it ensures all employees are provided with the necessary knowledge and skills to enable them to operate most effectively in the achievement of business objectives. Additionally, and as an investment, training should provide able employees with the knowledge and skills they will require in future assignments.

Beyond this, attitudes to training diverge. At one extreme is a commitment to encouraging the total development of the individual as a whole person, with open access to training and knowledge-expanding sessions, including self-development interests, some of which may not be relevant to present or future jobs anticipated by the employer. At the other extreme is the view that training should be focused narrowly on business performance improvement and have an early impact on the bottom line. This might be achieved, for example, by putting a training-cum-business consultant into a project team to improve project performance, but with no general concern for developing people. A good middle-of-the-road objective is that all training actions should be in response to legitimate, business-related training needs. As one consultant put it, 'If you think training is expensive, try ignorance'.

The role of training in personal development

The greatest part of a manager's personal development will take place on the job, learning from the boss and learning from doing, as he is progressively exposed to an increasing variety and complexity of assignments and new levels of responsibility. However, formal training is part of the management development process and, if it is carefully planned to complement each step of a manager's development, it can make a significant contribution to improving his current job performance and preparing him for further stages on his career.

All training must have a clear purpose and value. It should be designed to meet defined individual and company need. The design should be both time-and cost-effective and should take into account individual learning abilities. We must:

- Ensure that training adds value, and has a direct influence on business performance.
- Re-establish training needs at regular intervals.
- Design, or review and update, the content and form of all training programmes to maintain high standards of quality, and to meet training needs in the most cost-effective way.

- Endeavour to measure the effectiveness of training in relation to the required impact on performance.

Training needs arise from the requirements of the individual within the business, or from the business itself. The individual will identify training needs: to help him improve his performance in his present post and to assist in his preparation for a different or higher level position. The company initiates training in response to changing environmental factors which alter the objectives of a company and its managerial jobs, and the knowledge and skills required by its managers, and to respond to changing technologies or environmental changes which affect the ways in which managers will do their jobs.

At least once each year, a comprehensive updating and analysis of training needs should take place.

Individual training needs

A range of activities provides sources of data on the training needs of individuals. Most of these data are assembled on IDPs, where it is integrated into career plans such that the requirement is properly defined, the urgency established and provisional timing set. Most of the more urgent requirements will be scheduled for action in the immediate 12 months, while some longer term training related to future assignments may be scheduled for subsequent years. This great range of precisely identified needs will have to be summarized before a corporate training plan can be assembled.

An important contribution to IDPs, particularly regarding actions which may improve performance in the present job, comes from the performance appraisal process. This should provide a clear analysis of the individual's ability to do his job at the performance standards required. It should identify shortcomings in performance and what can be done to overcome them, and include agreement on specific training actions. Further, the appraisal discussions should cover the training felt to be necessary by the individual as well as his manager.

The other major contributor to IDPs will be the conclusions of the assessment centre and any other tests of potential. As part of the assessment of the ability to do other or higher level jobs, it is essential to identify gaps in knowledge, experience and competences, and to evaluate the extent to which training can fill these in. Actions which can be taken should be incorporated into IDPs, even if the appropriate timing is two to three years ahead.

As a supplement to the training needs identified to meet company performance and deployment requirements, individual growth objectives are likely to generate some further requirements. For example, there is an increase in the number of young people who want to obtain an MBA, and a parallel increase of external full- and parttime courses, many with company sponsorship. Most employers are willing to provide some support, even where the MBA is not seen as relevant to the individual's present work, because the enhancement of overall knowledge is attractive and increases the value of the inventory.

Corporate training needs

An organization capability audit based on business plan objectives and the changes expected in the environment is quite likely to identify factors which are expected to alter the operating environment and lead to a demand for new or different knowledge or skills, and which will require serious attention. The ways in which the necessary skills are to be acquired may involve a combination of external recruitment plus internal training, possibly in a relatively short time-scale. One issue where the training contribution will be critically important may be recognition that the company needs a rapid advance in its use of IT and that this is likely to alter the jobs of many middle managers.

Training needs analysis and priorities
The mass of detail on the training needs of individuals, plus the blocks of training required to meet corporate needs have to be analysed and summarized to produce an overall statement of the company's training needs and priorities. This will provide the justification for modifications to established company or corporate training programmes, the specifications for new programmes, and the numbers and levels to be covered, and will also provide the basis for booking individual training commitments in the immediate future.

A typical response on completion of an analysis of current (one year) training needs is that the company will need two to three years to get through it all. Sorting out priorities should not prove too difficult, but may involve going back to source material and judging the urgency of each element. Some of the larger requirements will stand to as essential and urgent while others will clearly be less so.

Any tendency to postpone or put aside training in identified requirements for aspects of man-management skills should be resisted. Many managers seem curiously reluctant to participate in training to improve their skills in counselling and interviewing, although these may be critically important to their effectiveness. Some of the largest and best-managed companies expect more than half of their total management training effort to be spent improving man-management skills.

The completed analysis provides the detail to be turned into training actions for the next cycle of 12 months, and is a critical element in the planned development of the manpower inventory.

Training actions

training is concerned with creating a rapid learning environment for identified groups of individuals with similar needs to increase their knowledge, skills and experience of predetermined activities, functions or behaviours. As people learn continuously from daily events, training should encourage more directed and intensive learning in specific areas, to bring knowledge up to a desired level, or performance up to a required standard, and should also enhance the individuals' learning abilities.

Training is work or activity related. Academic training or education has its emphasis on systematic intellectual teaching, the provision of a base of theory. There is no boundary between education and training-only a difference of emphasis-and some sections of training require an introduction to, or reinforcement of, basic theory. Once the needs are identified, summarized, and priorities determined, a programme of training actions can be developed.

Meeting the needs-how people learn

As the purpose of training is to impart knowledge or skills to those being trained, for training to be effective, some understanding of how people learn, or can be motivated to learn, is necessary. Training and leaning are two different things. To quote the old proverb, you can lead a horse to water, but you cannot make him drink'. In the same way, you can put someone through a training course, but you cannot make them learn.

If we want people to learn, we may need to provide encouragement and support for self-development. It may also be appropriate to assess their suitability for learning.

For example, entry to an academic course is likely to have an entry gate of successful completion of a preparatory or lower level course, which indicates an ability to comprehend the subject matter at the level required; an intellectual standard. Some training courses have (or should have) comparable entry gates in the form of an assessment of individual ability to cope with the training programme. There is no point in placing people on courses which are too advanced a level, and others may have intellectual limitations or some form of learning difficulty which may place them at a disadvantage.

The approach to teaching is of vital importance. It has been suggested that formal education systems tend to immunize adult students against learning; that much of what we learn as adults is picked up in less formal settings, or even by accident. This provides an initial pointer to the sort of learning environment and structure of training required to optimize learning by adults.

A situation where the trainer sees himself as the giver and the trainees as receivers in a junior schools sense is evidently not going to be effective, particularly with high ability people. The adult learner does not like to feel dependent and seems to want to take both responsibility for his efforts and full credit for achievements. He is likely to have strong views on his own training needs and how these may be met, based on past learning experiences. Ideally, he will want to be involved in determining the duration and content of learning and to be an active participant rather than passive recipient. He is likely to seek some measure of the effect or effectiveness of the training experience and will be influenced in his judgment by his degree of enjoyment of the process.

Action learning

The most effective form of learning from training at senior levels is likely to be some form of action learning. This can move much of the activity outside the training centre, although some theoretical input or grounding may be needed by this will generally be accepted if it is well presented with active, participatory discussion. The main learning is generated from questioning and problem solving, using case studies which are live and therefore very real and detailed. Action learning requires participants to work in small groups, and to clarify learning by questioning their individual learning objectives as a preliminary to team-working on these live projects. Learning is primarily by doing and from each other and, where possible, the team should be encouraged to carry the project through to implementation rather than present a conclusion and walk away. Learning from each other has several facets, from sharing experiences constructively, through interactions with team members, involving both criticism and advice, to reviewing with each other the lessons learnt from the agreed actions.

Involvement in real-life problems which require a solution and action alters the perspective enormously. By mixing training with reality, the learning process is enhanced. Realization that there is rarely enough information in complex real-time decision taking may be one of the key lessons. These real problems move training into the realm of development, because one of the best development situations is an assignment in a lively project team. The distinctive flavour of this training comes when participating managers are teamed with specially selected training staff, who operate as business consultants, to address real problems, and where the consultants support and steer the learning from within the project.

Learning in these situations is from demanding and practical experience, following which the students reflect on their observations and construct their own patterns of concepts or generalizations. The end result is a learning experience which may visibly pass through to the bottom line.

A learning culture

Ultimately, individuals will learn if they choose to. No matter how much effort is put into the design of training situations, if there is resistance to learning, the training will not be effective.

Resistance may stem from management attitudes and a voiced consensus that training is a waste of time. That sort of cultural resistance is not unusual and very difficult to dislodge, but it can be done. In a large construction group, identified a range of current operational problems which were clearly hitting the bottom line, and assembled a management training package to show in practical terms how some of these could be tackled. To fit the macho image of the senior managers, the course was designed to run for three 14-hour days, beginning on Sunday evening. The trial group duly arrived for what they described as their holiday-they dropped this phrase two hours into Monday morning. The involvement in new approaches to real problems caught their interest and we had to fight off demand for places on the programme until the top 200 managers had been through. And it really did have an impact on the bottom line.

In more enlightened organizations, the recognition of the value of learning is high. We emphasize learning, not necessarily training, because training is no more than one opportunity to learn. A learning culture encourages learning by everyone in the organization, and does so by producing many opportunities to learn but, more importantly, it encourages a way of thinking where everyone wants to learn and takes positive steps to do so which go well beyond any normal job related requirements. If there is a new development in the business, everyone wants to know about it, about the implications, and about the opportunities it may create elsewhere in the business. Expert help is brought in to run evening seminars, and everyone participates, in their own time.

This is the same attitude found in groups of high ability individuals who are dissatisfied with their present situation and are convinced that improvement is possible. It fits into a culture of openness and total encouragement for development, one that selects people who want to grow and then does more than just give them responsibility by creating an environment which maximizes their growth and development. Of course, you cannot just go out and create this in any ordinary company because it would terrify many of the residents but, as a vision to work towards, it is something for many human resource staff to savour and some to achieve.

Meeting the needs—structure of training programmes

Once training needs have been identified and priorities established, the means of addressing the requirements can be planned. The bulk of training in any large organization should be internal and local, possibly supplemented by corporate and external activities, depending on the degree of specialization and any one-off requirements.

The core of internal training will be essential preparation for the work to be done by the students at every level and preparation for advancement level by level, plus a range of functional, technical and man-

management courses associated with the needs of the overall business and the broadening of its managers. It will also instill an understanding of basic corporate values. Core programmes are likely to have an individually related to industry and culture and the corporate approach to development and training.

The purposes of the core training programmes is to ensure that individuals are properly prepared for the work they will do and for each major step forward in their careers and, where appropriate, to ensure that they acquire a common understanding of corporate culture and systems. Definitions of the basic knowledge and skills or competences which are essential for smooth transition to each new level provide the basis for the core training modules, from entry level through to middle management. There may be variations in core knowledge needed different streams; the core knowledge for all graduate entrants will be different to that for all finance staff, or all people with supervisory responsibilities.

At basic school leaver level, youngsters may enter a company or Government sponsored training scheme in preparation for work. Some of these courses may last several years, with a mix of further education and work experience, but may then lead into jobs which need the acquired skills but which have little or no promotion prospects.

At this intake level, there is likely to be some general induction covering the company structure, philosophy and general administration, followed by more specific training covering the industry, product familiarization, basic financial management and human relations skills, and company operating systems, depending on entry level. The pattern of training following entry is likely to be streamed by intake levels and functions, concentrating on the development of specialized knowledge.

Company requirements for career staff will require training in a further range of grounding skills, covering company systems, man-management skills and the basics of how to write a report, make a presentation and read quickly. There may also be finance for nonfinance people, marketing appreciation for all, and relevant technical briefings. Company culture is likely to come through strongly in these programmes, with particular emphasis on any new thinking, attitudes or behaviour felt to be critical.

As individual careers develop, the first supervision appointment should be preceded by a deliberate core of preparation, covering the continuing development of relevant functional skills and knowledge of financial systems, but with an emphasis on the development of man-management and leadership skills and also on the integration of learning modules into a comprehensive understanding of how the business works. This will fit into the manpower plans requirements for the relevant categories.

Later, the first managerial appointment should be preceded by a similar, but more advanced programme, with a further programme before the individual begins to manage other managers. At senior level, many organizations will look for development programmes outside their own boundaries, perhaps to group headquarters if they are part of a very large organization, or to the major business schools and management training establishments.

The detailed structure of each module throughout this range of training programmes needs to be built up from the identified needs and a knowledge of the targeted participants and how they are expected to learn. The form of modules should be variable. Provided that they meet the needs of the participants, the variation in the ways the needs they can be designed in an enormous variety of ways, being influenced particularly by corporate culture and both management and training staff preferences.

The introduction of any new corporate system, or a programme of culture change, is frequently backed up by training programmes which are more exercises in communication. Training can be thought of as communication with a specific purpose, and the use of training resources and techniques to present and sell new practices does create a learning situation which is legitimate. For example, the launch of an updated appraisal programme should be presented with strong training support. To be effective, these special programmes must be seen to have been started at the top, and to cascade down level by level, with all mangers seen to participate, giving everyone a common understanding and language.

Nominations for training

The selection of individuals at every level to attend any course must be evaluated carefully. Attendance must be linked to their agreed training needs and to their planned career development, corporate development and corporate manpower requirements. Further, the individual must be capable of understanding the training and benefiting from it. But, most important of all, is that the individuals must have a personal commitment to participate enthusiastically and to complete the intensive and demanding self-development opportunity which any training course provides.

Where appropriate, the nomination of a delegate to any programme should be timed to coincide with an anticipated job change or promotion, or some reorganization that will affect his duties and responsibilities. It is essential that participants should understand and support the objective. Attendance is normally sponsored by the immediate boss who has a responsibility to brief the attender fully and clarify the expectations. Attendance should never be a company requirement. There has to be choice for the participant and he must be committed.

The sponsor have a further responsibility; to ensure that their nominees do attend courses as booked, and are not distracted or withdrawn. Programmes are expensive to organize and run. Apart from the fact that the full costs should be charged when withdrawal occurs at a late stage, the opportunity to use that place for another individual may be lost.

On return from a training programme, the sponsor should debrief the participant to ensure the purpose has been achieved. The participant should be encouraged to do most of the talking. We find it useful to request a written report, giving a full assessment of the course and the learning obtained, and to follow this up after, say, three months, with the question, 'What have you done differently in the last three months as a direct result of attending the course?'.

Record of training

If we are serious about the objectives of training, and the purpose of each course, it is important to record participation so it counts in inventory analysis. For example, a number of companies will not promote an individual to the next significant level until their preparation-including participation in appropriate training courses-has been completed. Such organizations keep a note of individuals who are fully prepared for such promotional opportunities.

Completion of various specialist training prepares individuals for assignments which come up occasionally and for which a records search will be used to identify candidates.

A further application of training records is in the monitoring of the subsequent progress of groups, such as the class of '84, as this may provide pointers to the value and effectiveness of a sequence of regular programmes. For example, one company found that it retained virtually no-one from its main future managers courses after five years and discovered that, because the expectations raised were rarely met, participants saw the course as valuable preparation for job hunting and subsequently found themselves highly prized elsewhere in the industry.

Effectiveness

Training effectiveness is not easy to measure, but deliberate effort to evaluate training might lead to an evaluation of the following points:

Trainees' initial reactions: However carefully any course or seminar is designed and run, individual reactions vary widely, but the discipline of writing a short immediate comment on each session will enable any common responses to influence subsequent programmes.

Learning: Where the subject matter is clear, such as for specific inputs of functional knowledge, it is possible to get some measure of before and after proficiency. However, for most management courses the knowledge areas and levels are not definable with sufficient precision to use in this way, and one has to look at the use of knowledge and at behaviour.

Behaviour: Changes in job related behaviour may be evident, as in the construction industry case mentioned earlier. So too may be influence of training on particular competences. While these are evident in individuals, the use of newly acquired skills may be inhibited unless the surrounding managers possess and are using these same skills.

Organization behaviour: Where large groups of people attend the same or similar programmes, the reinforcement provided by many people trying out the same new ideas can lead to acceptance and consolidation. Measurement may still be difficult, but it is universally evident that certain changes have occurred. On a smaller scale, any team which has worked through a competitive live project will have been stimulated sufficiently to carry on with the project and use the skills they have acquired. If, when split up or returned to their original environments, they find their learning cannot be successfully communicated and absorbed, they will tend to revert to previous attitudes.

Evaluation can be attempted as people leave the training centre, but measures of effectiveness really need to be based on permanent changes in behaviour back on the job. The effect of the corporate culture on the use of acquired skills, and the influence of a wide variety of other factors, make it progressively more difficult to be specific about the impact of training. Ultimately, one looks at progressive improvement in corporate performance, and can attempt some judgment of the influences which have contributed to change, which will include training.

Apart from the effectiveness of the training itself, we should also analyse time. Many training courses are longer than necessary. With in-house training, there is no justification for padding and, because the training is designed to meet the specified needs of a known population, the content and format can be tailored to concentrate on essential material, to stretch the participants and to minimize the time required. Time is a critical cost element, as training costs should really include the total remuneration costs of participants while away from their jobs. Almost any factor which will reduce training duration will provide cost improvement.

6
Manpower Planning and Process

The first step in any planning effort is to get some picture of what has been occurring in a flow of people into and through and out of the organization. Obviously the past isn't going to repeat itself precisely, but some picture of the dynamic interrelationships among these personnel flows will help the organization predict its needs at least in the short run. Given past experience with managers leaving the organization, on the average, quit, retire, are discharged or become ill in management and managers promoting, the model predicates how many new managers must be hired at each level to maintain a stable system. The model can be used to predict the consequences of other contingencies. If more management training an more promotion from within is practiced, the model shows how much additional recruitment must take place at lower levels and how much recruitment can be reduced at higher levels. Similarly, if turnover can or should be reduced, the implications for reduced hiring are spelled out.

Manpower inventories and computers. The application of new technology to record keeping enables management to make more effective use of employee records in this regard. In addition to personal biographical information, such as age, previous education and training, work experience, and perhaps some psychological factors, such records contain a job history of the employee within the company. When such records are computerized, it becomes possible to answer quickly questions like the following:

How many employees in that jobs will be retiring in each future year? How many employees with appropriate backgrounds will be available for promotion to engineering management type of jobs next year? Who in our present work force is qualified today to be considered for an opening as a commercial underwrite?

Thus, skills and manpower inventories help to answer a range of questions extending from the broader planning type issue to immediate placement problems. The first requires a knowledge of the over-all profile of the current work ; the second needs specific, detailed information on individuals.

The profiles give management an "early warning system" for both bulges and shortages of people at certain points. Since there is usually a relatively long lead time required to get people through the system to reasonably responsible technical or managerial positions, appropriate selection actions must be taken years before the need will develop.

Good forecasting, combined with the use of flow models like the one we have been describing, can alert management to upcoming manpower shortages or surpluses. One the basis of such warnings, management can take measurement to handle problems before they become so serious as to inflict major damage to the organization. Below are two examples of the kind of problem that might be avoided were management given early warning:

The Delevan Company expanded rapidly during and after World War II, and few managers were hired during the 1950's and early 1960's. Thus, its managers are drawn from a relatively compact age group, and most of them are in their 50's and late 40's. There is little between them and the next group of managers, now in their late 20's and early 30's. Further, since the older managers "ran the show" by themselves for all these years, they have not developed the habit of delegating authority. As a consequence, to meet the needs of the 1980's and 1990's, and also to provide middle management in the interim, the company must (1) provide rapid development experience for the younger managers; (2) "pirate" qualified managers in their late 30's from other companies to till middle management slots; or (3) use a combination of these.

Sometimes even more drastic measures must be taken

As of 1977 there were a number of government laboratories which were in very much the same situation as the Delevan Company. A high percentage of their scientists were hired during and immediately after World War II. Since this was a relatively young group at the time, there have been few retirements or deaths. On the other hand, total employment has remained stable, so there have been few new recruits and most members of the work force are in their fifties or early sixties. Over the years a number of old-timers have declined in creative ability; some have narrow skills for which there is little need today. The newer skills are concentrated among the few young men recently hired. Now along come budget cuts and civil service requirements that heavy emphasis be given to seniority in layoffs. Given the age distribution of these scientists, even a slight layoff means that men with 10 or 15 years service are eliminated. Top management of the lab worries that if the cuts get deeper there will be no one left under age 55. With limited funds available, these laboratories do not have the options available to the Delevan Company to hire younger men. Instead, if government civil service regulations permit, they must encourage men in their late 50's to seek early retirement. Past trends often do not continue and new factors emerge which substantially modify the manpower flows. Then the more static Hairs model we have been utilizing is inadequate.

Changes in demand. Changes in the type of technology employed, in the range of products and services offered, and in over-all company policies will have an impact on future manpower requirements.

An insurance company begins making more widespread use of computers at the same time as it introduces job enlargement. Both have the same impact: a decreased requirement for unskilled clerical personnel. This, in turn, is bound to have an effect on hiring rates, promotions, and the costs of recruitment and training. But the precise impact is difficult to determine without the use of some sort of follow model.

Of course, such calculations are not easy to make. Equipment salesmen and technology enthusiasts often exaggerate the labour-saving results of new installations. Frightening predictions that computers would substantially reduce the need for white-collar employees proved unfounded. In part, of course, such predictions depend also upon sales forecasts.

As the Claridge Company shifts to a more technically sophisticated product line, it must anticipate that he proportion of college-trained salesmen will have to increase. However, the anticipated doubling of sales in these product areas in the next two years will not mean a doubling of manpower. The marketing manager for technical products will have to be consulted as to the relationship between sales volume and sales personnel.

Change in supply. Both a changing labour market and company policies can have a major impact on the supply side of the manpower equation. Perhaps college graduates are harder to hire or the government is placing pressure to hire more minority group members. Over the longer run, it may be realistic to prophesy greater utilization of women, minority group members, and even part-time employees.

It will also be useful to observe how the skills profile of the work force is changing over time. For example, if newer employees are better educated than older employees, the company can make use of more internal promotion to fill higher level positions. However, such a change may also be accompanied by higher turnover, since such employees are likely to have more attractive alternatives than do less well-educated employees.

Limitation of forecasting

Forecasting is still far from an exact science. While advance planning is useful in seeking to anticipate personnel changes which are just beginning to show themselves management needs to remember that such forecasts depend upon the continuation of trends, which may easily change. A decline in the economy can change drastically both the need for manpower and even the number of voluntary resignations. The result can be that a predicted shortage in certain jobs becomes a difficult surplus.

Given this discussing of manpower forecasting, let us now look at manpower planning in its broader sense. The manpower system consists of four elements: (1) job structures; (2) career paths; (3) policies to improve employment stability; and (4) policies covering work force reduction by means of attrition, layoffs, and discharge.

Job analysis and job descriptions

The job description is a source of basic information for all of manpower planning. In fact such descriptions are also essential for selection, training, work load, incentives, and salary administration, as will be discussed in forthcoming chapters. All these personnel areas require that the relevant duties, tasks, and employee requirements be made explicit for each organizational position.

Clearly, job descriptions are useful, even though individual deviations from them may be allowed. A new employee will want to know what is expected of him, and when the supervisor detects coordination problems between employees, he will need to know what each should properly be expected to do. Where such mutual role expectations are compatible, there is less likelihood of work flow friction.

Men's furnishings salesman: I get so angry, I could burst. Those stock boys are supposed to place the new merchandise in the display cases; instead they just leave the boxes all over the counter for us to arrange. They say it's our job, but I know it's theirs.

What duties are required in a particular position? The actual job title may be misleading. Some have been inflated to provide ego satisfactions, e.g., the plumber who calls himself a sanitary engineer. Others have just become less accurate because of technological or organization changes, e.g., engineers who have become technical sales specialists. Further, various individuals perform the same job differently. Smith is an accountant who enjoys spending time with lien managers, helping them analyze their cost variances; Jones prefers to stay with his own department doing analytical work.

Thus, there can be a number of ambiguities surrounding what is a job, but before dealing with the problems of definition let us look at us look at the process of acquiring and analyzing the relevant information.

Job analysis

Large companies have specially trained job analysts; in smaller organizations the supervisor develops the analysis, ideally in collaboration with the employees involved. The analysis itself consists of two parts: a statement of the work to be performed, and the skills and knowledge which must be possessed by anyone filling the job.

Job or occupational titles in themselves often give a misleading impression of the actual content of a job. A 'milk deliveryman," in addition to being able to drive a truck, must also handle customer accounts and sell the company's products. An engineer may have to spend most of his time *selling* department heads on the importance of using standard parts. Many so-called "clerk" jobs embrace a range of duties that are unrelated to the simple tabulating or recording activities one might associate with the job title.

Particularly at managerial and staff levels, the personalities of the key people with whom the new person will be dealing become an important element in any realistic job specification.

Care needs to be exercised that excessively broad and ambiguous requirements are not established like "intelligent worker" or "hard working" or "good personality." These encourage discriminatory or foolish hiring practices.

Job descriptions

Obviously there are a number of ways to group and organize duties and tasks, and these will vary somewhat, depending on whether we are talking about manual, clerical, professional, or administrative jobs. For purposes of simplification we shall simply list the major categories of analysis that might be included.

Functional categories	**And Examples**
Procedures, equipment, and quality subject matter with which job holder should be familiar; typical problems and requests he will receive	Develop new-product tests
Scope of responsibility; magnitude of discretion; "time span of control"	Responsible for approving claims up to $500, these decisions reviewed semiannually by Comptroller's Office
Standards of performance and work load	Undertake machining from blueprints to tolerances of .001 inch
Relationships; job interfaces	Calls set-up man to adjust equipment when tolerances can't be maintained
Supervision; reporting relation- work load	Reports to Purchasing Manager but also receives direction from comptroller and Manager of Engineering for special assignments
Qualification, probationary and training period	After 90 days becomes permanent employee

Working conditions, hazards	Operators must stand through most of the work day and be able to lift up to 50 pounds of machine sock; work in hot, humid areas under cranes
Promotion and career opportunities	Secretaries can quality for chief clerk and office manager positions.

If properly handled such descriptions could provide relevant inputs to computer controlled employee information systems that provide a variety of useful manpower data on, for example, the changing character of company jobs, similarities in tasks being performed in various departments that might suggest new promotional ladders or organization changes, and many others.

Ideally the description should distinguish between *prescribed and discretionary* content of each job. Thus, every salesman may be required to submit a field report weekly covering his customer visitations. More experienced and capable salesmen will be expected to use their discretion in providing management with information about changing conditions in the marketplace, its sources and possible remedies in terms of the company's product line.

As noted, management must decide how broad to make jobs; whether , for example, there should be a different category of job for each type of secretary employed or a single job, "Secretary." This can have a critical effect on promotion and transfer.

In much the same vein a decision has to be made as to how specialized or broad the job should be from the point of view of both selection and promotion. Narrow jobs are easier to fill, but they do not build as much qualification for future assignments, and they discourage the employee from reacting to emergencies or changed conditions.

The Carlton Company found that it could not get employees to do even minor maintenance on their machinery, because the job description made no mention of any responsibilities other than production. Management may be induced to keep the job narrow in order to reduce the evaluated wage rate that will be assigned. However, some supervisors will endeavor to collude with employees to upgrade the job in order to obtain a higher rating, thereby satisfying current employees and making it easier to hire new employees.

Of course, in dynamic organizations, where tasks are constantly changing. It may be useful to keep job descriptions more general, more flexible, and less detailed, particularly when they are developed by central staff groups to cover broad areas of the business.

An organization may wish to compare is job descriptions, or position guides, as they are sometimes called, with those developed for other organizations. The most comprehensive and widely cited reference in the field is the U.S. Department of Labour's Dictionary of Occupational Titles, which contains 22, 000 separate titles. More specialized management and professional job descriptions form representative companies are published by the National Industrial Conference Board.

Job specifications

Experience and judgment should enable the personnel specialist to help management translate job requirements into human requirements: the educational, experience, and personality requirements for anyone filling the job. This doesn't have to be a one-way street; knowing who will be available may exert an influence over how the job will be structured. The danger here is the temptation to ask for too much background in the way of education and experience, particularly formal degrees and certifications. These requirements can unduly increase salary costs and employee expectations. Similarly there may actually be advantages in bringing in new people who do not have a specific background in the field. We had always thought that a manager in consumer appliances had to have been in the business for at least four or five years. Now we find that if we take a bright employee from some totally different function of the business, he starts asking some very basic questions about how we do things, and doesn't take much for granted. Often those "dumb" questions about how we do things, and doesn't take much for granted. Often those "dumb" questions of the apprentice are just the kind of perspective our tradition-bound department needs.

It is difficult to specify personality requirements because of the measurement problem. Clearly some distinctions can be made in jobs that require building and maintaining close working relationships with many different people form positions that involve only routine contacts with a small number of nearby colleagues.

It is difficult to specify personality requirements because of the measurement problem. Clearly some distinctions can be made in jobs that require building and maintaining close working relationships with many different people from positions that involve only routine contacts with a small number of nearby colleagues.

Changing jobs to meet people's needs. Our discussion has assumed that job descriptions remain fixed and that people adapt in order to meet these requirements. While reasonable uniformity may be desirable in some situations, in others management needs to be flexible, as the following example illustrates. We very much wanted to keep Miss Callaner. She had a number of attractive outside offers and wanted more responsibility, but we thought she just didn't have the math and statistics background to take over the Market Research manager's office. Then we finally decided to upgrade the department's statistician's job to where he became "Assistant to the Manager." Since she would have less to do with survey design and evaluation, we were able to add more liaison duties with our field sales departments to Miss Callaner's new position. In the process we think it's probably a better mix of duties of a Market Research manager than was the old job.

While this type of analysis is often used to reduce the skill requirements to make positions more suitable for minority group members, the same approach encourages managers to think creatively about the whole range of job-person relationships. Particularly within management there can be a number of alternative "clusterings" of duties to assist in the matching of people and jobs.

Designing career paths

Every organization is faced with such questions as: Should employees be promoted within relatively specialized carrier lines or be given broad exposure to a variety of jobs? How much promotional opportunity is desirable? Under what circumstances should openings be filled with an already trained outsider or by training an insider?

The answers depend upon an understanding of the dynamics of promotion systems, including organizational needs and employee expectations.

Employee expectations

Within a given organization, its members come to anticipate a certain pattern of job progression based on what they have observed of the internal mobility of other employees. Below are some examples of quite different types different types of career ladders:

In police departments it is expected that everyone starts at the bottom, as a rookie, and moves up-even though there has been some recent discussion of bringing in college men at higher ranking status as "police agents."

The military traditionally has a two-career ladder system: an enlisted man starts as private and advances as high as warrant officer; an officer starts as second lieutenant or ensign and may end his career as a general or admiral. But there have been increasing opportunities in recent years for some enlisted men to become officers.

The hospital has an even more rigid caste system: nurses aides rarely become nurses; nurses may aspire to be head nurses or even superintendents of nurses, but never doctors, etc.

The university for its academic staff has a well-known ladder: instructor, assistant professor, associate professor, and full professor.

Typical companies have at least four distinct ladders:

— manual workers are hired into unskilled or labour pool jobs and promote on the basis of seniority up to higher paying and/or easier machine-tending positions, or perhaps inspection.

— skilled tradesmen often start as apprentices, or "helpers," and move up to craftsman classifications.

— clerical employees move to more desirable locations and higher paying while-collar jobs.

— managers often start as trainees or as assistant supervisors and can, of course, move to top management. Often there are separate ladders for sales, production, or engineering which converge for the last few steps in upper management. There may also be separate "professional ladders" in fields like accounting, law, and personnel.

Characteristics of career paths: length and breadth

Very obviously the rookie patrolman can move up a much longer career ladder than a hospital medical records librarian, who, in most hospitals, will occupy a "dead-end" job-i.e., one that provides no promotional steps. Most industrial relations experts favour the formal structuring of jobs to provide reasonably long, orderly career ladders, because of the motivation and training they provide.

Where the career ladder leads up to jobs that are much different or much more responsible than those required at the port of entry, special care needs to be taken to be sure that hiring standards reflect this. Thus, petroleum refineries traditionally promote personnel form the labor gang up through many steps to the stillman post, a crew chief responsible for millions of dollars of technical equipment. There can be morale problems associated with new employees being overqualified for their port-of-entry job, marking time until they can be promoted to positions that call for more of their abilities.

On the other hand, in industries like advertising and in many research and teaching posts, while salaries and status go up with movement along the career ladder, there is little difference in the type of work performed at the higher, as compared to the lower, levels. In fact, in many engineering companies, an employee may shift from being a manager of one project to a staff technical person on the next project.

Some companies rely so heavily on the promotion-from-within policy that they cannot afford to keep people who do not qualify or are not desirous of moving ahead. Many universities similarly follow the practice of "up or out," which simply means that instructors and assistant professors must either earn a promotion or seek employment elsewhere.

Breadth of job or career paths vary substantially. In more craft-and professionally-oriented work, the paths tend to be "narrow" and the experience obtained is all in similar function. Many modern managements, on the other hand, pride themselves in providing very diverse exposures to rising executives. Managers shift laterally as they move upward, gaining experience in a variety of functions such as marketing, manufacturing, and finance. Other companies find that while this circuitous routing makes a well-rounded top executive, it tends to diminish the in-depth knowledge and competence of executives in the various functional fields. They, therefore, keep the lines narrow until close to the very top of the pyramid.

Broader career paths increase the likelihood that there will be few or no "dead-end" jobs, because a wide variety of promotional opportunities are made available. A more broadly and less parochially rained work force with wider perspective can be the result. Against these advantages must be weighted the costs of constantly retraining men for new jobs requiring different knowledge and skills.

Technology shapes career ladders

The breadth and length of career ladders can be related to the technology of the industry; it is no simply a management judgement. The manner in which employees move from one job to another is largely determined by he industrial structure. The automobile, steel, and aerospace industries offer examples of quite different patterns.

Dead-end paths

Many times employees are concerned that the promotion ladder on which they find themselves doesn't lead "upward" very far. "In this organization, if you get started in Packaging, you know you've had it."

The organization needs to guard against a situation in which pockets of promotable personnel build up in some areas where promotions are "sluggish"-and a dearth of promotable personnel builds up in other areas where promotional opening are more numerous. It is desirable to have "many roads to the top" so that no group is favoured. Where technology is changing rapidly, this may be difficult to accomplish, and only a major retraining and development program can project promotional opportunities.

"When the computer industry shifted from vacuum tubes to solid state components, a large number of traditionally trained electrical engineers who had been qualified to move to high-level positions found themselves "disqualified" because of their lack of knowledge about solid state physics, just as several years before that, the mechanical engineers had been displaced by the electricals!

A seemingly innocent change in management policy within a given department sometimes wipes out the promotional opportunities of a while group of workers. Whyte describes such a case:

In view of the rapid scientific and technical development of the company decided that only college graduates should be appointed as foremen. The new ruling hit the HI-Test plant particularly hard, for some of these men had been singled out as especially able and promising...They were at the top now with no place to go.. It was common to hear them say, "We're just bumping our heads against the ceiling here."

When management finds that there are dead-end jobs in the organization where promotions are unlikely, it should try to tie them to other jobs or else fill them with employees who have neither the capability nor the desire to move ahead. Without promotional opportunities, organization effectiveness may suffer.

Manpower hoarding: Departments sometimes try to hoard more employees than they need, particularly employees with scarce talents; for example, engineers were hoarded during the shortages of the 1960's. Understandably, employees grow restless when they realize that the opportunity to advance is being blocked by the piling up of surplus manpower. Excess manpower can mean absence of job challenge; if there are too many people for too little work they get into one another's way.

Interdepartmental competition may also be a factor in restricting promotional opportunities. For example, a department that was carrying on a full-scale training program for tool-makers refused to honor requests from employees who finished the course to accept a promotion to another department, claiming that the other department was "too cheap" to do its own training. On the other hand, there are situations in which everyone recognizes that certain departments will train workers for other departments. The important thing is to insure that the organization's control systems, such as cost accounting, reflect this contribution. Also if some supervisors are reluctant to let their trained workers move on to higher-rated jobs in other departments, serious inequities are bound to develop.

A means of minimizing some of these differences among departments is to require that job opening be announced throughout the organization and candidates be evaluated by some screening body that is not partial to those coming from a given area. This practice, sometimes called "open bidding," serves to tie together a number of individual promotional ladders.

Clarity of career paths

Some career ladders are sharply defined: the head teller is always selected from senior tellers working in her bank, who, in turn have moved up from trainee to teller. Others are less so: In company X the most common route to the presidency has always been through sales, but the most recent top executive had a financial background and currently there are rumors that the Board will bring in someone form outside the company.

There is one obvious disadvantage of clarity in career paths. Some companies are able to transfer ineffective employees to less critical jobs or to positions which don't block others from obtaining promotions, without this appearing to be a demotion. Particularly in large organizations, it is possible to create reasonable ambiguities as to whether a man is going up, sideways, or down. Often salary levels are not known precisely, and even when they are, there is usually enough flexibility in most salary evaluation plans to allow for more generous payment to longer service employees who are no longer eligible for promotion.

Whatever their "shape" or clarity, career paths must be integrated with other aspects of personnel administration. They must be related to the salary structure so that each promotion provides a significant salary increase. Also the various lines must be compared with one another to be sure that there are equitable interrelationships. An assistant department head, which is two rungs up one career line, should have similar pay and responsibilities to other assistant department heads who are similarly situated.

Internal promotion Vs. External recruitment

The above discussion of career paths assumes that the organization is intending to fill most of its job vacancies through internal promotion and employees will gain their qualifications through on-the-job training, perhaps supplemented by additional format training. An alternative policy would be to recruit a candidate for higher level openings from outside organization, someone already filling a comparable job in another firm or with the appropriate formal education. What criteria are available for choosing between training and selection as alternative means of filling job openings?

Thus, the filling of any single job has many ramifications. The proposal here would cut off promotional opportunities for some personnel and increase them for others. In addition, training costs would go up, a least in the short run, and conceivably the company would have to pay higher salaries to recruit college personnel. All of these factors would have to be weighed before a final decision was reached.

The case for promotion form within

Providing better-qualified employees. No organization can rely on outside recruitment to fill all its requirements. True, certain jobs are similar from one organization another, but most jobs require specialized knowledge that can be obtained only within a particular firm. Even jobs that do not seem to be unique require familiarity within a particular firm. Even jobs that do not seem to be unique require familiarity with the people, procedures, policies, and special characteristics of the organization in which they are performed. As we have already observed, career lines allow for on-the-job training insofar as jobs are arranged in such a way that experience gained performing the lower job prepares one for the next rung up.

Internal recruitment is also a means of selection. The most selection procedures, such as interviewing and testing, provide, a far from perfect picture of a new applicant's potential worth. Seeing a man in action, however, over a period of years, enables management to make a realistic assessment of his skills.

Promotion also provides a process of "selective socialization." Over time, those whose personalities and skills enable them to fit into the organization's human relations tend to stay on; those whose personalities conflict tend to leave-either voluntarily or involuntarily. This is called-self-selection.

Providing motivation: People will work harder if they know this will lead to promotion. But employees have little motivation if the better jobs are reserved for outsiders.

Providing job satisfaction: Americans want to keep moving ahead. Being given additional responsibilities is not enough; people want the tangible recognition that a higher-ranking title provides. In addition, most workers look forward to unbroken, continuous service. They like to feel that they can get ahead in their own company without having turn elsewhere.

Cost: It probably is more expensive to recruit an outsider who has already demonstrated high performance and must be lured away form his present employer.

The case for recruitment form outside

Just as many organizations seek outsiders to sit on their boards of directors in order to introduce new perspectives, so they reserve certain lesser positions for newcomers. This infusion of "new blood" keeps the system from growing stagnant, repetitious, and overly conformist. This is probably of less importance in hourly-paid jobs than in staff and managerial jobs, however. Recruitment from outside the firm can reduce the expense of training new employees, which can be very high, particularly for skilled craftsmen and technical personnel.

Different company philosophies: The recruitment vs. promotion decision is partially one of economics: where do you invest your money? Recent research suggests that companies tend to adopt unbalanced strategies: Some invest a great deal in expensive selection testing techniques, while others are more likely to have extensive on-the-job training and stress promotion from within. Rarely do companies have what would seem highly desirable: a balanced program.

Unless expanding very rapidly, most companies are more likely to hire highly trained professionals from outside than to promote their managers from within. However, if, as many observers suggest, management itself is becoming more professionalized, we would anticipate increased job hopping among impatient executives. Anxious to find challenge and increased responsibilities, they may seek out alternative sources of employment to climb a career ladder in contrast to moving up within a single organization.

Administering career paths

This has been a conceptual discussion; now let us move to some of the difficult day-to-day problems of administering these "lines" and "ladders."

Number of promotional steps

The number of promotions possible is not inherent in the technology; management makes the choice. For example, take a clerical department with 20 employees doing various telephoning, typing, filing, and copying tasks. By deemphasizing the differences in job duties, the company could place all jobs in the same salary grade. Contrariwise, by meticulously evaluating differences among the jobs, conceivably each employee could receive a slightly different salary. In the latter case there could be a 2—step promotional ladder.

What is the optimum number? Too few promotional steps may injure morale by eliminating the sense of personal progress and accomplishment. Too many promotional steps may mean that an excessive amount of time and effort must be spent in selecting candidates gaining acceptance for the choices, and shifting employees. The result may be chaos. In approaching this question of frequency of promotions, we must be careful to distinguish between promotion to a better job and periodic wage or salary *merit increases.*

There is a good bit of ambiguity particularly on professional jobs, about when an employee has actually moved to a more important job, for job definitions are often quite elastic. An engineer, for example, may be required to work on a more difficult assignment for several months before the change is officially recognized by what we would call a promotion-that is, a job title with more prestige and increased income. When a man is officially promoted to a more responsible position may be simply a matter of supervisory judgment.

Varying attitudes toward promotion: People differ in what promotion means to them. Many managers tend to project their own feelings about promotion onto their employees, forgetting that not every employee wants to be promoted-at least not in the terms in which management typically conceives of promotion. Employees differ greatly in their "level of aspiration."

Management sometimes makes the mistake of using a highly unpopular job as the required stepping-stone to higher positions. As a result, serious shortage may develop in these higher positions because few candidates are willing to spend time on the undesirable rung of the promotional ladder.

Similarly, when an employee enters into an apprenticeship program he is often required to accept a reduction in pay for a number of years before he wins a craftsman's rating. Management officials assume that employees should be willing to make short-run sacrifices in return for long-run benefits, but they forget that their own time perspective may be quite different form that of their employees.

What management regards as a substantial promotion may not seem like a promotion at all to the employee himself. The nurse or salesman may not want to be an administrator. The additional responsibilities or travel requirements of some jobs may more than outweigh the status associated with the new salary and title. In another situation, technical personnel may be reluctant to give up their specialities to become administrators. In order to motivate and reward these professionals, many companies establish "dual ladders" dual ladders" which allow them to move up through a series of steps without assuming managerial positions. Although this does alleviate some of the inequalities, it is doubtful that, given the present organization of industry, the same status and perquisites, can be given to a "Principal Research Scientist" as to a "Divisional President." The promotional ladders are not really parallel.

Finally, there is always a group of employees what are quite content to stand still, who prefer the known to the unknown. Unwilling to risk what they have in hand, they want to stick close to the people they know and the responsibilities they are familiar with. To these people, improvement means regular wage increases, more security, and perhaps and easier job. Yet in some industries, technology has made it difficult to satisfy this last desire; the majority of jobs are fast-paced and demanding.

Management must provide career ladders that will encourage promising employees to take the risks involved in moving upward. It must not discourage valuable employees from seeking advancement by making service in an unpopular job a prerequisite to promotion. It must provide for employees who do outstanding work but are unwilling to take on new and additional responsibilities. And it must provide alternatives for those who are reluctant to assume supervisory responsibilities.

Selecting who is to be promoted

Having settled on a general promotion program management must face the still more difficult task of deciding who to promote, since there are usually more candidates than openings. The choice usually revolves around evaluations of relative merit, ability, and length of service.

If promotion is to be an incentive, the best-performing employees ought to be advanced. However, since differences in merit may not be readily measurable, the man who was not promoted may feel that favoritism was involved. As a further source of discontent, on many jobs performance reflects the coordinated activities of many people or chance factors-this making individual merit difficult to measure.

But there is also the question of ability-that is, potential performance on other jobs. Jones may be doing fine on his present job but lack the ability to do the work on a higher-ranked job. Smith, on the other hand, may be doing poorly at present because of inadequate supervision or the unchallenging nature of the work. Put him on more difficult work and he may blossom.

Long-term factors are also relevant. The individual best fitted for an immediate promotion may not have the greatest long-term potential. That is, the most deserving candidate at the moment may seem to be a senior employee who has the ability to move only one more step up the promotional ladder, but it may be better to promote a younger man who may eventually advance into higher management.

In addition, ability is as difficult to measure as merit. The specific traits, attitudes, personalities, and skills that make up ability are frequently ambiguous. For this reason companies often rely on objective measurements-years of education, for example.

To complicate matters further, some people may be given special opportunities to acquire valuable skills whereas others are not. Certain jobs give employees an opportunity to move about freely, bringing them into contact with high-level personnel whose opinion are crucial in promotion decision. They "learn their way around the organization" and are on the spot when a promotional opportunity turns up.

What we are saying is that some effort should be made to reward both merit and ability, even though neither is easy to measure. Organizations that have failed to reward excellence in service, or that have relied too heavily on personal relationships or length of service, suffer in terms of both efficiency and morale.

Seniority

The extent to which promotions should be based on

seniority is almost always an area of dispute between unions and management.

Arguments for seniority: The use of such criteria as performance evaluation, selection tests, and supervisory opinions leads many employees to feel that promotions are not made fairly. And charges of favoritism and discrimination may lead to declines in morale and productivity. Unions object that as long as managers have the power to select the most suitable candidate for promotion, is a simple matter for them to discourage ambitious employees from speaking out against company policy.

To avoid this difficult, it is often suggested that promotions be based on some objective criterion, and that the only objective criterion is length of service. When management known that it is going to promote the employee with the longest service, chances are that the company will give him the training he needs to move into the new job. Management will also tend to perfect its initial selection procedures, for once an individual gets into the organization his future will be relatively assured.

In certain societies, the older men invariably occupy the highest positions; although we do not follow this practice rigidly, we still feel that it is appropriate for the senior people within an organization to occupy higher positions than their juniors. True, we make a good many exceptions: the long-time employee who is clearly incompetent, and the young man who is a genius. However, ours is at least partially an "age-graded society" where age, position, and prestige are correlated.

Arguments against. Excessive emphasis on seniority, however, may violate employee attitudes about the "right" way of getting ahead: Indeed, the promotion of incompetents solely on the basis of length of service clearly violates another strongly entrenched cultural attitude that rewards should be somehow commensurate with accomplishment.

The top-skilled members of galls-and steel-making crews are typically men who have worked their way up through a lengthy, informal apprenticeship system, in the old days they worked long hours, often without pay, under the far-from-tolerant tutelage of a craftsman who would put up with his younger assistants only in return for numerous services. It was a long, hard, grueling road to the top, and those who have made it frequently resent the rather automatic manner in which men can now work themselves into similar positions primarily by accumulating seniority.

Contribution to ability: Up to some point, it seems likely that the longer an employee works a one job, the more qualified he becomes for promotion to the next-higher job. Research among production workers suggests that the employee with the longest service often is better prepared for promotion than management is initially willing to admit. For many jobs, particularly hose at the lower levels, differences in ability from one employee to another may be less important then noting the most senior employee to another may be less important than management tends to think. Consequently, the gain in morale derived from promoting the most senior employee may more than offset any slight loss of efficiency.

But the correspondence between seniority and ability undoubtedly diminished as length of service increases, and beyond a certain level, continued service brings very little gain. Indeed, after a point, increased length of service on a given job actually *reduces* an employee's ability to change jobs, producing in him what is often referred to as "a rained incapacity to learn"; that is, he becomes so imbued with the problems and procedures of his present job that he is unable to adjust to new circumstances and situations. The expert becomes simply too expert in what he is doing.

Reward for loyalty: In a sense, to grant promotions on the basis of seniority is to reward employees for loyalty. In an organization that wants to keep to its employees and avoid costly turnover, a type of guaranteed promotion plan may be an effective personnel policy. Traditional Japanese industry believed this.

No one would deny that loyal service deserves reward. But the question is how many loyal employees become discouraged about their future with the organization when hey realize that they can be promoted only as fast as length of service permits? Also, the emphasis on longevity induces a "ritualistic devotion to duty" in which perfection in the small things, the job routines, and the avoidance of mistakes take precedence over imaginative and energetic pursuit of more challenging goals. Further, those characteristics that were most associated with job success at lower skill levels may not be as useful in higher level jobs. Balancing this, however, is the reduction in destructive interpersonal competition that can occur when there is too much uncertainty about who will be promoted.

Striking a balance

Every organization must decide on the relative weights it will give to merit, ability, and seniority in making promotion decisions. Even when company policy or the union contract sets up merit and ability as the prime determinants, many an organization succumbs in time to the presumably more objective criterion so seniority. Supervisors in general believe that relations with their subordinates will be easier if they promote the most senior employee. Almost all companies give some weight to seniority in practice, although firms that are unionized give it greater weight than those that are not.

Administering the promotion program

Dealing with the individual

Handling employees who are unlikely to be promoted. A boss must be able to predict what members of his group will be the most likely candidates for promotion when openings occur. And he must try to keep those who are unlikely to be promoted from taking it for granted that they will soon be moving up the ladder. For example, a long service employee may assume he is promotable even if he is not. If his boss allows that misapprehension to continue, the employee will be sadly disappointed when someone else gets the job. And if his buddies encourage him to think that he is wronged, he is likely to create a serious problem.

Problems of this sort can be avoided if the boss makes a point of discussing with the hopeful candidate the exact nature of the new responsibilities long before the opening actually occurs. Then, if the employee is clearly not qualified for the promotion, he may be brought around to accept his unsuitability. The supervisor may be able to suggest a way in which the employee can supplement his background or improve his performance of that he will eventually become eligible for a promotional opportunity. If he shows himself unwilling to make the extra effort required, the job of winning his assent to being "passes over" becomes much easier.

Dealing with the employee who doesn't want to be promoted. In our culture, anyone who odes not want to advance is regarded as somehow queer or lazy. Many individuals take on higher-level jobs even when they are not suited for additional responsibility; but the cost is high to themselves and to the organization. In fact, people who really should not be promoted may come to feel that a failure to show interest in advancement is a black mark against their record. Actually, a clear recognition of each employee's psychological and intellectual limits is valuable both to the organization ad to the individual.

The employee who has reached the limit of his ambitions or abilities still has a vital role to plan. The armed services have discovered the value of long service "old-line" master sergeants who stay with a particular unit, providing stability and continuity, while its commissioned officers come and go. So, too, employees who have been in one department for a long time may help to break in newcomers, particularly new supervisors.

But nonmobile people must not be permitted to monopolize the training jobs in which more suitable candidates can be prepared for higher positions.

Helping the successful candidate. Serious problems are experienced by the man who does move up into a new position, particularly if it involves supervision. Unless he has been with the group for a long time, and unless the group has resistance. His new subordinates will be uncertain at first about what his new leadership will mean to their future.

The employee who is promoted to a nonsupervisory position has his problems, too, for he may be facing new responsibilities for which he is not wholly prepared. Nothing is "automatic" in a strange job, and the new man is under great strain. In worrying about what he should do and how to avoid mistakes, he many become so tense that he performs clumsily or forgetfully. If his supervisor is aware of these strains, he can provide the understanding that will help the new man over the hump of the first days on the job.

Craft consciousness

Where promotion ladders are short and narrow, employees are more likely to perceive the job as being a part of their personal property or territorial preserve. Any threat to an element of the job situation becomes a threat to the employee.

This is one of the primary sources of resistance to technological change; the employee is reluctant to see his work modified for fear of his job status. His income, his security derived from knowing everything there is know about the job-any or all may be threatened.

Craft-consciousness-the feeling that no one should work outside his narrowly defined job duties-has traditionally been strong in the construction and maintenance trades. A carpenter will refuse to do any work by carpentry, and he will refuse to let other employees do carpentry work-even if this means that other employees must stand idle or be laid off.

Other groups that lack the traditional craft status of the building trades try to erect barriers around their particular skills. The primary motivation seems to be job security, for workers feel that if they can prevent other men from doing their work, they will be able to make their own jobs more secure. Unions in general encourage craft-consciousness, because they look upon it as a means of restricting management's power to make transfers. And every time management gives in to a union demand to make craft boundaries more sacred, a past practice is established, which is in a sense frozen into the union contract.

In one company, machinists were prohibited from picking up any material that had fallen on the floor. This was the janitors' work! Even valuable parts were sometimes swept away by the cleanup crews because the machinists refused to pick them up.

Management itself, by carrying specialization and division of labour to extremes, may be responsible for proliferating an unwieldy number of narrowly defined jobs. Where jobs are defined narrowly, each with a limited number of highly specific duties, the problem of shifting employees is accentuated. Employees, taking their cue form management, then proceed to erect artificial barriers that inhibit flexible transfers designed to expedite the flow of work and to even out work-load inequalities.

"I am the only girl in the office who can run this mimeograph machine. It's not easy, let me tell you; it's old and has got lots of tricks to it and it takes years to learn. I don't want other girls using it; this way I know they really need me around here. When we occasionally run out of work on the machine, I don't think its fair for me to have to do other odd jobs. After all, this is what I am getting paid for."

Reducing craft-consciousness. How can management deal with excessive craft-consciousness? First, by accepting as natural the work group's efforts to protect its members. Very little is accomplished by accusing employees of "feather bedding", for employees are anxious to strengthen their "property right" in their jobs.

A second way of meeting this problem is to develop job description that define jobs in terms of the work that needs to be done rather than in terms of abstract craft skills. In short, determine job duties by the requirements of the work process, not by traditional concepts of what a craftman is.

In inducting new employees, the supervisor should try to instill in them the broadest possible definition of their jobs. A good recruitment and training policy helps, for employees with diversified skills and good training are more easily transferred.

Transfers

Not all movement is upward. Particularly where career ladders have substantial "breadth", employees many shift sideways. To be sure, the transfer that is a lateral move may involve greater salary and responsibility, but there may also be times in which the individual accepts an assignment at a comparable level in order to broaden his experience or in order to get around a "blockage" in his career ladder. Transfers are also used by management to cope with incompatibilities between the job and the person holding the job. When an employees has trouble doing his work or develops personal friction with his boss or fellow employees, the answer may be to transfer him to another job. Remedial transfers, however, are often used as a means of glossing over serious problems. Where the manager is arbitrary, where newly hired people receive inadequate training or where is arbitrary, where newly hired people receive inadequate training, or where employees discriminate against members of minority groups, it is far better to resolve the problem directly, rather than postpone it through a transfer. After all, the replacement for the man who is transferred may face the same problems again.

Nevertheless, when technological change is introduced or customer demands change, then the manpower needs of some departments may decline while the needs of other departments expand. To safeguard the jobs of long-service employees and to avoid losing the skills of trained personnel, most companies try to transfer employees to other jobs. Moreover, a company that follows a liberal transfer policy and provides retraining for employees who are transferred to new job has less difficulty in introducing changes.

Good evidence of intelligent manpower planning is stability of employment. Erratic "ups" and "downs" in employment levels, expedient hiring, substantial overtime during periods and layoffs and short workweeks in others, are prima facie evidence of poor planning. Well-managed companies seek to avoid hiring surges and plan for cutbacks far enough in advances so that *attrition* will bring employment levels down to efficient levels.

Many companies take great pride in their policy of resisting layoffs and providing stable employment. They claim it pays off in a more secure work force, more loyal to the organization, and less fearful of management changes costing jobs. Obviously a utility or a company fortunate enough or skilled enough to create a stable market for its goods or services finds such a commitment easier to make and keep than a company facing cyclical markets.

There are many incentives to encourage management to provide stable employment.

Many state unemployment insurance plans, as well as company-sponsored supplementary benefit plans, are designed to penalize the employer with a record of unstable employment. In addition, the process of laying off and rehiring is expensive to administer, and valuable employees may eventually be lost to other employers. Change in employment levels involve expensive shifts of workers within and between departments. Just the fear of layoff may encourage employees to consider "stretching out the work" as they mark time, waiting to see "who will be the next to go." Disagreements over seniority criteria result in costly, time -consuming grievances, as do intergroup arguments over short workweeks.

All these possibilities provide a stimulus for the firm to seek means of regularizing employment by using techniques such as the following.

1. Trying to develop a more flexible work force through

careful selection and training, supplemented by contractual provisions that permit relatively free transfers between departments-though craft consciousness makes this more difficult.

2. Using temporary employees or overtime in peak volume periods.

3. Taking on additional products or service lines whose variable demand will complement the demand for existing products-for example, if peak demand occurs in the summer, seeking products that are used primarily during the winter.

4. Exploring the possibility of warehousing goods during periods of slack demand, and offering new incentives for customers to stockpile during normally slow periods or order longer in advance.

5. Contracting out work that would require the employment of new people who might not be needed when the job is completed-for example, maintenance or construction work.

Merely listing alternatives, of course, is an oversimplification of the problem. Temporary personnel agencies typically have higher hourly rates than employees can be hired for directly. Overtime, when continuous, can lead to employee expectations concerning future earnings levels that may be unrealistic and cause resentment when the overtime is reduced. Also excessive overtime reduces efficiency. Inside employees can also resent "losing" work to outside contractors. Among the problems encountered in transfers are the resentment associated with being wrenched out on one's normal work and routines and familiar social group. Also the employee may complain, and often legitimately, that the temporary work is more difficult and is beneath his accustomed status. At the very least the supervisor has to be sure that his earnings are maintained and that if the temporary work is distasteful, such transfers are shared equally.

Whatever its policies or intentions, most organizations at some time do have to face up to the painful decisions surrounding a reduction in the size of the work force.

Reduced employment

Management must provide orderly pathways downward as well as upward and seek to minimize the personal and organizational disruption with cutbacks in employment. If the cutback is a small one, the least painful method is *attrition*, allowing normal turnover, retirement, and cessation of hiring to bring employment levels down.

Reduced Hours or Layoffs

When instabilities in work load persist and attrition is not adequate, then the next choice is usually between shorter work weeks for everyone or laying off the least senior employees, keeping the remainder full employed. Sharing work which is what reduced working hours implies-means in effect that unemployment is distributed equally. Depending on circumstances, this may or may not be an advantage to the firm. Sometimes the exact procedure is specified in the union management agreement, thus making desecration impossible.

What criteria does management use in deciding which procedure to favour? The nature of the industry itself is a critical factor in this decision. A department store could not arbitrarily reduce the hours it is open to the public without seriously damaging its business. Other firms have more flexibility in resorting to a reduced schedule when business warrants.

Naturally enough, longer-service employees are

likely to press for the laying off short-service personnel, in an effort to secure higher income for themselves. The availability and the magnitude of *unemployment insurance* benefits may also influence the choice between laying off employees and reducing work hours. At some point it becomes more desirable, from the employees point of review, to accept these insurance benefits and avoid the travel expenses taxes, and effort associated with reporting to work for relatively brief periods.

Seniority vs. Merit in Layoffs

When business is poor and costs are relatively high, management becomes more sensitive to productivity issues. It is regrettable that such slack periods alert management to problems that have probably existed for some periods of time. Layoffs are usually more painful to employees in such a periods when other companies may also be experiencing cutbacks because alternate jobs are scarce.

The first temptation is to dismiss marginal performers, say the bottom 10 per cent in terms of existing appraisals. In fact, this is done in many organizations. However, where there is a union or where very long service employees are involved, there are a number of impediments to this policy.

Most employees and their supervisors will assert:

"Look, James was here almost 20 years before they discovered his work was unsatisfactory. Sure, we know he wasn't the best by any means, but don't you think the company could have noticed this and have done something about it a lot earlier? Now he's got family responsibilities and debts, and a man in his late 40's can't just step into another job that easy if these layoffs should last for long"

Of course, almost every industrial union makes sure that its contract with management includes a clause requiring that employees be laid off in reverse order of their hiring: last hired, first to be dropped.

Ambiguities in counting years of service. But even with the acceptance of this principle of length of service governing such manpower decisions, the question remains as to how seniority is "counted." Here are some alternatives:

1. Company-wide seniority: the length of time an employee has worked of the company.
2. Department seniority: the length of time an employee has worked in a particular department of the company.
3. Job seniority: the length of time an employee has held a specific job in a particular department of the company.

The method used obvious has a significant effect on the choice of which employee is laid when, for example, there is a surplus of clerical in the Accounts Receivable Department.

The "youngest" employee under formula 1 might be a recently hired stenographer in the Engineering Department to take the job of the laid-off stenographer.

The employee with least service under formula 2 might be a secretary who has been with the company for several years, but who recently transferred into the department when an opening occurred.

Under formula 3, the company would be required to lay off the youngest employee doing the specific clerical job in the Accounts Receivable Department where the surplus existed.

Bumping. Let us introduce another complication:

bumping. The application of seniority may mean that a whole series of moves is generated when a single employee is laid off.

Let us look again at our earlier example. Under formula 2, the following would be a more typical sequence of events: The Account Receivable Department has too many stenographers. The stenographer with the least service in that position would lose her jobs. However, she would have the privilege held by an employee with less department service than her own. Thus, the girl first displayed might "bump" a tabulating clerk with less service. In turn, the tabulating clerk may bump a file clerk with even less seniority than hers. And the process repeats itself as long as displaced employees can find other workers with less seniority than themselves occupying jobs that they are able to perform. Larger companies find that cutbacks in manpower may generate thousands of job shifts, which in turn create massive record-keeping and personnel problems. Shifts of this sort are bound to provoke countless grievances and complaints about alleged inequities in the demotions.

Selecting from among Alternative Seniority Systems

Which seniority system is best form the point of view of the firm? Though there is no simple answer, the following criteria may help management in arriving at a solution.

Reducing frequency of movement. One criterion to apply in evaluating a seniority system is whether it reduces the frequency of job-shifting. Shifts create grievances, and they also give rise to training and efficiency problems. Although management may require that an employee be able to perform the job for which he exercises hi "bumping" privileges, it is hard to measure performance. Under the pressure of events, employee job shifts inevitably result in workers being displaced from jobs which they do efficiently and being placed on jobs for which their performance is marginal. "Bumping" works best when the movement takes place down a promotional ladder and where everyone in the department has worked place down a promotional ladder and where everyone in the department has worked his way up from the bottom jobs. In summary, to satisfy this criterion, management often favors a relatively "narrow" seniority unit, such as job or departmental.

Retaining valuable employees. The use "narrow" seniority units may be costly to the company, however. Assume that the need for machinists has declined temporarily. Under a system of job seniority, the company would be required to lay off machinists with long training and experience. Then, if these machinists accepted jobs elsewhere, expensive recruiting and training would be required to acquire new machinists when business picked up. Obviously, management would like to shift these employees to other jobs, and allow less valuable employees to be laid off. Many times some form of department seniority is a good compromise solution to a problem of this sort.

Encouraging requisite mobility. "Narrow" seniority units discourage employees from accepting transfers, for they lose their seniority when they transfer from one unit to another. Thus," wider" seniority units make it easier for the company to provide a flexible work force.

Swift return to normal production. After the need for layoffs has passed, management seeks to return to normal production as quickly as possible. Naturally, key employees must be the first to be recalled. The seniority system usually specifies that those who were laid off last will be called back first. Presumably the more senior workers will have held the more important positions.

This correlation is not always a perfect one, however, and management may seek to recall junior employees whose skills are essential to the resumption of production.

Employees desires. Management also wants to be fair. But what is fair is not easy to determine.

In theory, employees and unions favor "wider" or more inclusive seniority units than does management. They argue that it is unfair to lay off employees with 15 years of seniority in one department, when there are employees with only one year of service in another department. Unions have sometimes sought corporation wide seniority agreements to enable an employee whose job is terminated in one company location to shift to another; on occasion, they have even demanded that moving expenses be provided.

In actual practice, employees very often favor narrow units much as management does, only for quite different reasons. Because the employee tends to consider his job as a piece of "property", even though management has a very different interpretation, he seeks out the help of his fellow workers who share the same or nearby jobs to help him protect his valued possession.

The importance of seniority and the careful calculations of self-interest that go into employee decisions impinging on this area are revealed by the following case:

Either management or the union may seek modification in existing seniority regulations when changes in technology or in the company's business threaten widespread loss of their jobs.

The Furst Corporation is eliminating is consumer product lines. Under the terms of the existing union-management agreement, even employees with 30 years of service expecting to retire in six months or a year will have to be laid off since the seniority clauses forbid interdepartment "bumping". Recently hired young men in adjacent departments will retain their jobs while these senior employees are separated.

These are very delicate problems of equity and contract. The union finds it difficult to decide what to ask the company, because inevitably some of its members will be injured and others will benefit.

Termination or Layoff

Management has a responsibility to inform the employee when a layoff is assumed to be permanent. Many union-management agreements and company policies specify that an employees' right to be recalled, with a priority determined by his length of service, will not continue beyond one or two years. Thus, if the layoff persists for this length of time, the employee also loses his claim to other employment benefits associated with accrued service. If he is rehired, he will come back as a new employee. Many companies pay a *severance or termination* allowance when an employees loses his hob through no fault of his own.

An alternative to dismissal for older employees is early retirement, an option which is being used with increasing frequency particularly by relatively profitable companies. Realistically they compare the cost of maintaining the employee through to normal retirement at full salary with the additional cost of a more generous early pension.

A systems approach to manpower planning

During recent years the terms *human resource management systems* and *manpower planning* have come to the fore. Their usage reflects a growing concern for personnel systems as distinct from compartmentalized personnel policies. An other way of saying this is that there is growing awareness by managers and personal specialists that the organization is an *organic* entity. All of its parts are so interdependent that a change cannot be introduced in one place in one place without affecting the total.

One of the unfortunate legacies of the scientific management tradition was the encouragement given to managers to compartmentalize their problems. Just as the job of the managers was divided up by the fathers of scientific management into separate components, there is still a tendency to classify personnel problems into watertight categories.

We have a shortage of people qualified to be sales managers: This is a recruitment problem.

Too many engineers are requesting a transfer out of the power division: This a transfer problem policy.

We are losing many of our best craftsmen that have been hired in the last several years: This is a turnover problem.

In fact, every one of the above designations may be incorrect. What appears to be a changed recruitment requirement may, in fact, be a training problem. Excessive transfers may reflect inadequate pay or promotion procedures, and turnover can be symptomatic of the same or other defects in internal personnel policies.

In the effort to identify the underlying manpower system that shapes the flows of personnel through the organization, personnel research analysts examine critical comparisons. For example, comparisons like the following may be useful in examining the background and career patterns of those who quite, those who are asked to leave, and those who are promoted.

Do engineers who quit during their first three years

of employment graduate near the top or middle or bottom of their class?

Do we lose more young managers who begin their careers with us in our trainee program or more who go directly to a first non-training assignment?

How do the internal company careers of staff people who go "up" rapidly differ from those who promote more slowly?

Traditional management thinking often involved a search for simple cause and effect relationships. Poor performance must mean poor selection procedures. Absence of qualified candidates for a middle-level position must mean poor promotional policies. In practice, it is rare to find such simple causality operating. More often they result from a complex interaction among a number of company processes, including, supervision, remuneration, career paths, performance appraisal, and others. The managerial challenge is to identify the interrelationships among these various organizational processes. Such analyses do not automatically tell the organization what it has been doing right and wrong, but simply what has been happening. However, such new understanding can play a highly useful role in decisions concerning promotion, management development, and selection policy.

Another example of the significance of interrelationships is provided by the manpower implications of various job-security provisions, such as guaranteed annual wages or sub plans. On the surface these appear very costly since they penalize management heavily for layoffs and job insecurities. But these costs have to be balanced against potential benefits to be derived from a work force that feels more secure and, therefore, may be more willing to accept new technology and job changes.

Manpower planning requires management to assess the total impact of existing company procedures on the utilization of manpower. It is not unusual to find organizations failing to recognize that the impact of a given personnel policy depends upon its interaction with other company policies; there is no such things as separate compartments for remuneration, selection, promotion, etc. Decisions made by individual department managers ramify throughout the total organizations.

Companies may have a non-discrimination policy in employment, but unless it is backed up both by suitable training of supervisors and effective monitoring, such policies may be ineffectual. Similarly a great deal of effort may be devoted to selecting high potential graduates of technical schools, but if placement and promotion policies do not reward their abilities, it is likely that the effort placed on selection will be vitiated.

A manager may be reluctant to promote anyone to a middle-level position in his department who does not have a unique and narrowly defined experience; yet this job is a critical stepping stone to broader, general management positions in the company. His immediate needs for fully qualified personnel may have to be modified in the light of the larger organizations' needs.

We cite examples like these to emphasize the need for synthesis and integration in viewing management decisions and policies. Too often their values or "correctness" are assessed independently one from the other.

Long-run vs. Short -run Cost and Benefits

A manpower planning approach to personnel problems should also counter the tendency of all managers to neglect long-run consideration. An investment in training may not pay off for may years and not until the employee has moved up to other jobs. His present manager can be disinclined to "invest" in the future when his incentives motivate him to look only at the present. The organization requires some process by which these longer run considerations can be factored into today's decisions. As in all planning, that is the contribution of manpower planning-to make sure that choices are made today which will assist the organization in moving to the objectives it has set for tomorrow.

A Definition of Manpower Planning

Manpower planning then is an integrated view of the personnel systems of the organization, which allows individual managers to make improved day-to-day decisions that will be consistent with the total organization longer run needs. Its successful operation requires:

1. An understanding of the existing interdependencies among personnel systems and personnel flows.
2. The establishment of guidelines and policies based on this understanding within which managers will make their personnel decisions.
3. Some mechanism to detect when these policies either need changing or are being violated.

If this is done successfully, the organization will be in a better position to decide such questions as :

1. Where should begin hiring people?
2. Where should we reduce hiring and allow attrition to decrease the size of the group?
3. Where should promotion rates be accelerated, slowed down; similarly where is more training required, less?

The process

The purpose of manpower planning is to provide continuity of efficient manning for the total business and optimum use of manpower resources, although that optimum utilization of people is heavily influenced by organization and corporate culture.

Manpower resources include the intellectual property of the company and the possessors of its core competences, potentially the most easily lost or misused properties, and the most in need of thoughtful planning. As manpower planning is concerned with manning in the business, it cannot be a stand-alone activity, but must exist as a part of the planning process for the business itself. The lack of suitable manpower can place severe restrictions on the ability of a business to achieve its objectives, which highlights both the importance of realistic manpower planning and the need for it to be fully integrated with the overall business planning process.

Like any other process, manpower planning has numerous elements and the process will not work efficiently unless the full range is used and properly integrated. The same applies to business planning, within which manpower planning should be viewed as a subset of elements in the overall system.

The manpower plan itself falls into two parts—the determination of the manpower required to run the business at a series of points in time into the future, and the means of supplying those requirements. For the planning to work well, believe it is important to examine the full demand and supply position so that optimum solutions can be evolved. This is not limited to central or specialist activities, but should involve all line managers fully in the review of options.

The review process, which brings needs and supply together, is frequently given insufficient and attention. This may be because once all data are brought together, the result can seem complex and difficult to grasp, but any reduction in complexity is achieved only by ignoring some of the data and taking a limited view, which could reduce the potential for achieving the most effective resourcing.

The purpose of the comprehensive periodic review is to consider all of the needs across the business and to match these with the career preferences and development of the people so that a complete pattern of decisions can be devised for the resourcing actions anticipated over the months ahead. This review provides abase of preliminary decisions for all following actions regarding people. There may be sound reasons for a subsequent change of decision, but then the options and alternatives which were considered in the review provide a starting point for the fresh assessment. If some new requirement emerges, the considerations noted in the original review should help define the updated options quickly, and the implications of alternative actions. Should the scale of unplanned change be extensive, a fresh review might be initiated, at least locally.

In the review process itself, the management task is to balance the many competing and sometimes conflicting elements. Some examples might be:

- conflicting demands for available research and development resources at peaks of activity, with an excess supply available during troughs;
- inbalance of skills emerging as technology alters the product range; and
- uncertain timing of developments, which affects the timing of deployments.

These reviews cannot anticipate situations which develop at short notice, but should take into account the need for flexibility to cope with the manpower implications of events such as intended future acquisitions, new business opportunities not allowed for in plans or retention actions needed to avoid the loss of key individuals which might damage established plans.

The review process may be viewed as the master programme which integrates resourcing activities with business planning at an operational level to ensure that organization structures and the preparation of manpower resources are matched with the manpower requirements necessary to achieve business objectives and respond to a changing and possibly hostile environment. In parallel, the process should optimize the utilization and growth of the human resources available. The emphasis in most reviews may be on the short-term (one or two year) actions, but there must be a longer term (three to five or five to ten year) perspective—particularly for management continuity, which is a special section of the same process—as the lead time for supply can require this notice.

Meaningful manpower plans are only possible if the review process brings together all of the relevant information at regular intervals and uses these data to reexamine, at every level, the relevance of present and planned future organizations and the competences which will be required against those available. Outputs from each review should include: detailed decisions on future organization changes and anticipated manpower deployments for a period through to two to three months after the next scheduled review; outline decisions on longer term organization changes, deployments and culture change plans; plus confirmation that business requirements can be adequately resourced (or not).

All manpower supply plans and actions should stem from this process and should incorporate provision for continuous reappraisal to identify fresh problems, to respond to new or changed needs, and then to implement actions or monitor progress towards action. This is essentially the means of driving the process of effective resourcing within the business and involves management at every level in a network of associated decisions and action.

Preliminaries to review

Reviews require sound preparatory work and comprehensive personnel records which give accurate and objective data on all employees. We cannot make judgments on the supply of particular skills unless we have sufficient data on the skills possessed by existing employees. Building up full records requires both an effective system and determination to ensure the data are complete, up-to-date and accurate. Also, the information must be in a form that facilitates easy access during a review.

Personnel records can be seen simply as raw data and their contribution to reviews may come more from analyses of the overall inventory of personnel. Any flaws in that inventory, identified before the review begins, provide part of the review agenda. For example, heavy loss rates for a key employee group can be analysed carefully in advance, so that part of the action agreed in the review addresses the identified problem. Or, a progressively worsening distortion of the age profile of a category may need to be tackled.

Analyses of the manpower inventory and of flows can establish whether problems are developing which are likely to affect required manning levels, and should play a key part in preparing the agendas for reviews. Equally, as other agenda items emerge, analyses may offer potential solutions.

Manning standards and utilization

The whole manpower planning process depends enormously on the base of manning standards. This will start with what exists and what should be, and take in all of those factors which will change current standards, including by how much and when. Without some measures of this sort, meaningful planning is very difficult. Many organizations start with what exists now and refine the position as they identify the separate forecastable categories, the bases for assessing standards and the rates of change.

Manager, supervisor and employee involvement and interest is needed to determine standards of all sorts; the first-hand measures they have of the utilization of people are key factors in planning forward needs and subsequent implementation and control.

Ideally, manning standards should be developed from analysis of essential work requirements, with some form of productivity measurement wherever possible. Measurement is by no means restricted to direct manufacturing operations-it can also be applied to many office or support functions. Where local attitudes or management style make straightforward measurement difficult, existing data in the hands of supervisors and managers can provide useful standards which will encourage supervisors to improve their own human resources utilization, thereby improving manpower productivity.

Wherever this type of analysis is carried out, opportunities should be sought to restructure and enrich jobs and to match people's abilities to job demand, thereby raising the level of job satisfaction. With this comes lower manpower loss rates, lower absenteeism and tighter manning standard generally.

For all this, existing standards have an inertia which we must try to overcome. If we aim to improve the use of people in partnership with subordinate supervisors and managers, we may find the secret of radical improvement in overall manning quality as well as number. This is an area for experimentation to determine what works in your environment.

Manpower requirement planning

Manpower requirement planning follows on from the establishment of the main assumptions in the business plan. Once we know the level of sales volumes and mix, the manufacturing schedules required, the research and development programmes, etc., we are well on the way to establishing the matching manpower requirements. The plans should include built-in assumptions about the organization structures to be used, and their effects on the levels of manpower required.

Plans should be set out with schedules of associated manpower requirements, giving precise categories, skills and levels for every function. This detail will be necessary as a starting point when the question of supply planning are tackled. Where appropriate, requirement plans should be based on manning standards associated with work demand factors to facilitate modification as volumes or systems change.

Manpower information systems

Modern management depends on having comprehensive data on which to make decisions. For any system, specification of required inputs and outputs is essential. In building up the manpower database, full coverage of traditional personnel records is required, and it is increasingly possible to cover sophisticated elements, such as competences required for effective performance of a job, and the competences possessed by individuals. Data on absenteeism and overtime are also part of the system.

Who are our employees; what skills do they have; how good are they; how are they developing? These are just some of the many questions to which we need answers. Much of the analysis should come from the information system, but the current inventory is altering all the time with recruitment and losses, promotions and transfers. Assessing the rate and form of change in the inventory is vital to questions of manpower supply because, what we cannot provide from within, we must seek out from other sources.

Data on appraisal of performance, assessment of future potential and the use of psychological tests are all part of the information we use to get the answers we need.

Flows

Analyses of the patterns or flows of people through parts of the organization are invaluable to the manpower planner; flows provide the major part of out supplies data and identifying changes in flow patterns can point to possible difficulties, such as when an existing flow pattern becomes insufficient to meet a changing demand.

Flows tell us about the availability of people who are ready to advance to their next career stages and also provide information such as the average rates at which individuals progress through jobs, and how those rates vary for different types of people in different functions.

Manpower supply planning

This is the crunch point where we bring together all the

data we have on our future requirements, and on our present manpower stock and the ways we expect it to change. From these analyses, we see the future manpower supply set against the developing inventory, detailed by function, category, skill and level. These show our future recruitment needs, highlight needs to increase the promotion rates of some categories by intensive training and development, show retraining and redevelopment needs and identify excess staff who are likely to become redundant.

In all of these areas, we need action programmes to ensure that we meet our recognized needs. We must be sure that the actions required are taken and are successful. Otherwise, basic assumptions on the provision of human resources within the business plan may be adversely affected so that business objectives are endangered.

Manpower control and audit

The philosophy throughout this book is one of planning ahead, but this requires basic controls and audits. The logic of controls on every aspect of manning should be evident. We are dealing with an expensive resource that can be easily misused or underutilized. Controls should be low key, yet quietly ensure that we continually try to use those resources in the best ways possible, and do not causally add additional and non-essential resources. Controls are exercised current actions and decisions.

Subsequently, we audit results to be sure that intentions have been achieved and that decisions have not been overlooked or ignored. This happens far more than we expect where there is little or no audit. In the whole area of management development in particular, and across the spectrum of planning following the review process, ensuring that plans are followed through is essential. If this is not done, there is little benefit from the considerable use of valuable time involved.

Management manpower planning

Above a certain level, manpower planning ceases to be a matter of numbers by category, and becomes linked to individual positions and individual incumbents. For the top slice of the company, we are dealing with a combination of business development, organization development and individual career development. It must be handled with considerable care, by unbiased and imaginative executives; it must also take into account the employees' viewpoints and preferences, and involve them fully if it is to be a workable plan.

Corporate culture

How a company is managed, its organization structure, its manning standards and thinking on 'how we do things around here' are all determined within a corporate culture. Any significant change in efficiency is almost certainly going to be culture related, but culture is both difficult and slow to change.

If the business demands a change of pace or efficiency, or a different way of doing things, it is not going to come about solely from planning changes in manpower standards or utilization. There will be a need for some radical action to change what people accept as norms for many aspects of their work behaviour, which may well result in a severe disturbance in current manpower and organization. We will examine aspects of culture and manning standards elsewhere in the book.

Periodic full reviews

The way reviews are carried out is likely to vary enormously from one enterprise to the next, but the principles should be more uniform. The most critical of these is involvement. All of management should participate, with the lowest levels contributing their parts first and progressive reviews forming a reverse cascade up through the organization structure, finishing with a review of the overall manpower plan and the management continuity position at the top.

At the bottom end, each manager should discuss requirements and deployments with his direct subordinates. Then he can prepare for the review with his boss. A reasonable target time per level might be three weeks, if planned early into business diaries. As reviews progress up the structure, they should concentrate on the continuous two or three levels in the organization, progressively dropping off the lower levels as the reviews progress upwards. However, issues thought to be of concern at higher levels will be carried forward, such as skills shortages which may have an impact on the business.

The supporting paperwork will vary, with much being prepared as working noted by the participating managers, but it is sensible to assemble and retain some basic record of the discussions and agreements to enable progress to be monitored later, or as the starting point for fresh consideration if an unforeseen development occurs. There might be sections in the notes for:

- business and environmental changes;
- organization and manning reviews; and
- human resource action plans

The first section should record the business situation and assumptions on which the review was based. The notes might include a brief appraisal of actual business progress against the business plan, and changes in the environment which differ from the assumptions in the associated environmental scenario, followed by updated views and an evaluation of the implications for human resource management.

The organization and manning plans section should concentrate on: the immediate organization structure, including any fresh thinking on its evolution; the filling of all senior positions at each review level, both currently and in the future, including preparatory development; and reviews of manning specifications, standards and levels, and how they may change. It will be useful if all the main assumptions made in the plan are recorded, so that any need for changes has a firm base on which to build.

The third section, covering human resource action plans, is a smaller scale replica of the human resource action plans, and will include reference to major human resource strategies associated with the achievability of business objectives. There should be notes on progress against the milestone in current action plans, plus details of any new plans triggered by new business or environmental developments, and the associated human resource implications.

A final section in the notes might cover implementation action, with details of plans to prepare individuals for fresh assignments, implementation of training plans, and a whole host of action points, covering individuals or groups, designed to ensure timely resourcing.

Frequency

The frequency of this process should be determined by need. One company in a rapidly changing high-technology sector runs through it at quarterly intervals with strong line management support for what they see as sensible discipline which keeps their organization and manpower utilization finely tuned. In less dynamic industries, a major annual review plus a less formal, but ongoing, midyear update may be sufficient.

The drive to carry through the review process must come from the top and from the line, who must recognize its value to themselves and to the business or they will not spend the time doing it ! The human resource function may need to provide some of the drive plus some strong supporting back-up. Reviews compete for management time and must demonstrate their contribution to business development and profitability. Local management is generally supportive if the process is working properly and they can see value for their efforts but, even then, resistance to allocating sufficient time may arise as a result of operational pressures.

Essential actions triggered by these reviews, such as manpower movement between divisions, may be difficulty to arrange without the involvement of higher management. Usually, these moves need to capitalize on knowledge of the immediate business and be local to those business areas the individuals concerned know well. Movement should generally be within functional disciplines, so that the fast learning is limited to the new business area.

Application to individual decisions

The periodic in-depth manpower review establishes a scenario or framework of preliminary decisions. Following this, there will be many day-to-day actions to take before gaining a final overview and implementing the decisions. For example, a chain of individual moves and appointments may be planned to follow a retirement. These should be under scrutiny as the implementation time approaches and they would normally be implemented in a straight-forward fashions. However, one of the links in a chain may fail. Someone may resign, performance may falter, or other events may change the situation, causing the plan to be reshaped.

If circumstances change, the obvious starting point for fresh consideration should be the notes from the previous review supporting the original intention, which may record the options and contingencies considered. It is logical to go over this ground in detail, starting from the original review. It should not be acceptable to take a fresh ad hoc decision which is quite unrelated to the careful and wider ranging considerations which took place in the review process.

Actions involving changes from plans should require the discipline of reference back to the comprehensive discussion. For example, a decision to send someone on a training course should fit into his longer term development plans; secondments to meet an emergency are unlikely to have been planned far ahead, but should match a need to broaden experience; a change to a career plan may have been proposed on the basis of one incident, but should be viewed against the full assessment and track record; and so on.

Perhaps the most serious unscheduled actions occur when a key person resigns, or when an unplanned business opportunity requires an immediate appointment. One such appointment was followed by a chain of seven other changes down the line, severally disturbing an entire plan. If that happens, a fresh examination of that sector of the business becomes a necessity. Indeed, any event which triggers a significant volume of unscheduled deployment changes should be followed by a full review to assess the degree of weakness caused and the actions which can be taken to reinforce the reserves of management.

7

Principles and Evaluation of Training

In India considerable importance has been accorded to training in social development and this is evident form the fact that the community spends roughly six million dollars annually on training every year. Obviously while few would deny that training is essential, there is considerable doubt about its optimal contribution to development. There are complaints about the ineffectiveness of training and possible waste of resources because of the use of stereotyped and conventional methods in training which are often not set completely in tune with job requirements.

On the one side there is pressure of training a large number of functionaries, on the other there is an urgent need for improving the quality of training. One of the reasons for this is that very little time is devoted to planning of a training programme. The organisation of training is based on certain assumptions which are need-based to be substituted in accordance with new concepts of training. The following are four common assumptions implicit in current training practices placed in comparison with another list of assumptions which appear to be more useful.

A continuous process

Training is a continuous and life long process. Right form the time a child is born he starts receiving training form his mother for a variety of needs, so that he becomes a social being. His training continues in the school and the college situations. However, training as an organised effort is designed with certain objectives, for example, to help the trainees to be informed of the subject matter which they have to use in their work situations. Apart from change of attitudes, their skills have to be improved and knowledge or information has to be imparted through effective methods. In other words, training provides and atmosphere of sharing and synthesizing, with the help of the trainers, the information already available on the subject. Training is a time-bound programme. Thus, there is a separate specialized discipline of trainers specializing in the field of human activity.

Education, perhaps, is the only field where there are trainers who train teachers. For instance, a person with M.Sc. degree in child development, nutrition or social work becomes a work. They may have the subject-matter knowledge but are not trained during their university education even at the post-graduate level on how to transmit this knowledge to the students or trainees.

There has been in some quarters criticism of training and it is often argued that personnel can acquire administrative capabilities and work skills through apprenticeship rather than through formal training. While the training cannot by itself guarantee the success of a development programme, its untrained personnel are unlikely to prove effective. It is in this context that experts, administrators and planners greatly appreciate the relevance of training in development process.

While planning for training, limitations inherent in the training process are generally not given any serious consideration. Some people feel that training does not produce any lasting impact on the final outcome of the development process. However, the results of training do not become visible immediately. Training largely brings about an increase in one's knowledge but change in

Prevailing concept	*New concept*
1. The acquisition of subject matter knowledge by a participant leads to action.	1. Motivation and skills lead to action. Skills are acquired through practice.
2. The participant learns what the trainer teaches. Learning is a simple function of the capacity of the participant to learn and the ability of the trainer to teach.	2. Learning is a complex function of the motivation and capacity of the individual participant, the norms of the training group,the training methods and the behaviour of the trainers, and the general climate of the institution. The partici-pant's motiva-tion is influenced by the climate of his work organization.
3. Individual action leads to improvement on the job.	3. Improvement on the job is complex function of individual learning, the norms of the working group, and the general climate of the organization. Individual learning used, leads to frustration.
4. Training is the responsibility of the training institution. It begins and ends with the course.	4. Training is the responsibility of three partners: the participant organization, the participant, and the training institution. It has a preparatory, per-training, and a subsequent, post-training phase. All are equally important to the success of training.

attitudes and behaviour manifest slowly. Moreover, knowledge and skills can be taught or transmitted in some degree. Perceptibility and tact can also be developed through training.

Organisation

The organisation of training involves a four-step process:

a) The identification of needs

b) The formulation of training policy and objectives

c) The implementation of training policy.

d) The assessment of effectiveness.

Identification of training needs

The first step in determining training policy is the identification of the agency's needs for trained manpower, both present and future. The basic questions in the regard would then be:

i) What kind of jobs are to be done by the trainee?

ii) What specific skills should be developed among trainees?

iii) How many people will be needed to do them?

To answer these questions management needs to be able to say how it expects the agency to develop. When and estimate has been made of the jobs to be done to satisfy both the present and foreseeable objectives of the agency, the skills required in the main occupational categories need to be recognised. The requirements of individual jobs need to be kept under review, so that training can be adopted to the needs of the agency as they emerge, since changes in the work process often call for skills that may differ from those originally envisaged.

Formulation of training policy and objectives

The amount and type of personnel required and for which

recruitment and training policies are formulated; recruitment, selection, training and re-training are all part of the process of matching as closely as possible the manpower available with the present and future needs of the agency. In a development programme many types of personnel may be required and if the programme is extensive, the number required may be large necessitating additional inputs for training in the form of train-ing infrastructure, etc. In such a situation, the programme has to be phased out in accordance with a scheme formulating the policy of training, its specific objectives, period of training, cost estimates.

Implementation of training policy

Achieving the objectives in the form in which they are finally approved involves planning, organising and implementing appropriate training programmes. The agency will have to decide which of the tasks involved will be allocated, in whole or in part, to the training staff and which to others.

These are:

i) Planning

ii) Further education

iii) Organising and implementation

Application of systems approach to training

There should be systematic approach to training and an instructional system should be developed, keeping the short-term and long-term objectives of training policy in view. This, requires a systematic procedure for the development, implementation, evaluation, revision and constant review of training in order to adjust it to changing needs, and policies.

Assessment of effectiveness

In order to justify the cost and efforts put in the training, the effectiveness of the training has to be assessed either internally within the agency or externally by an outside agency. Whereas the internal agency may monitor and evaluate the programme at regular intervals to introduce corrective measures in the light of specific objectives, the evaluation may be done also by an external agency after reasonable span of time to make an objective assessment within the parameters of broader objectives.

Evaluation

It may be useful to examine why training programmes do not always exhibit the desired end- results. A relevant cause could be the tendency to lay more emphasis on the form or method or training than on the specific goals which are sought to be accomplished via the training activity. A reason why training programmes, generally, do not succeed in imparting adequate skills is the failure to distinguish between knowledge of the process and training functions performed.

Training risks

A training programme may suffer from the following risks:

Design risk. Among the several reasons leading to inappropriate design are the following:

i) Training to deal with some symptoms and causes;

ii) Training content and targets influenced by prejudice;

iii) Internal and external trainers preferences;

iv) Limited search in the choice of materials and methodology.

Conduct rise: In the actual conduct of the training, even with a good design, the following may be some of the possible risks:

i) cancellation of some or more of the planned training events;

ii) failure to get nominations;

iii) failure of the nominees attending the course;

iv) non-availability of faculty members of their substitutes;

v) absence of inability of the Course director in integrating the inputs by different speakers towards the achievement of the goals; and

iv) administrative lapses.

Learning risks. The level of learning could be at risk from the following factors:

i) lack of interest in learning;

ii) no perception of either awards for learning or punishment for not learning;

iii) negative attitudes arising from personal and work role experience.

iv) complacency and resistance to self-change;

v) Sense of helplessness about self and others in the organisation in utilising training inputs.

Transfer risks: The stage of transfer may be found to suffer form the following difficulties:

i) lack of interest of the individual trainees;

ii) lack of support form his superiors;

iii) partial or no implementation by group of joint commitments to action.

iv) turnover of the trainee:

v) wrong posting of the trainee;

vi) lack of coordinated approach in strategy, organisation and systems; and

vii) other environmental crises.

A view-point is sometimes put forward that often the trainers have great difficulty in determining the kind of training needed for and what they expect it to accomplish. At the same time, it is extremely difficult to evaluate the results of such training. However, the fact remains that the evaluation in respect of training as related to trainers has been ignored more than any other area in training. Methods of training have not been always properly evaluated. The fact that this evaluation like any other evaluation is a complex effort should not be a deterrent for making all reasonable efforts in evaluating whether or not such training is worth the corresponding effort of the trainer.

Evaluation of a training programme/course is very important not only form the point of improving training but also to help the participant trainees and trainers to function more effectively. Evaluation can be involving the total programme or it can be partial aiming at appraisal of some salient aspects.

Purpose

a) To find out the extent to which the objectives of a course/programme have been achieved or are being achieved.

b) To examine if the course contents are relevant and fulfilling the objectives.

c) To assess the efficacy of the training methods and to improve the same.

d) To evaluate general atmosphere in the class, field placement, other physical arrangements, duration of training etc.

e) To study the extent of participation by the trainees.

f) To study the entire programme or a part of it form the cost effectiveness point of views.

g) To see that the instructions are conducted in a manner consistent with the system as it is planned and designed.

Components to be evaluated

There are many components of a training programme. An evaluation aims to determine the effectiveness of each.

Kinds of evaluation

From the view of the agency undertaking its evaluation may be:

i) Internal if it is made by the agency implementing the programme.

ii) External if an external agency is assigned the job.

Types of evaluation

Pre-course evaluation

i) Evaluation conducted at the entry point in the course is known as pre-course evaluation. Questions regarding the knowledge and skills could be listed and trainees asked to answer so that the trainer knows the level of knowledge and skills they already possess.

ii) Trainees should also list their expectations in the order of priority.

iii) Areas in which the trainees would like to learn more or further improve their skills should also be indicated at the beginning to improve programmes. Pre-course evaluation helps in planning the course to meet the specific needs of trainees and include such area that help them to perform better in their jobs. But the problem here is that the information collected at pre-course evaluation may not be very reliable.

Each of the above categories of evaluations have their own purpose and focus depending upon what the training agency is looking for.

In the following paragraphs, different types of evaluation in training situations are described:

Concurrent evaluation

One approach to evaluation may be to ask the trainees themselves to evaluate the training programme. It can be questioned, however, on the ground that it is difficult for the trainee to be objective and that they are in to position to judge efforts of such and evaluation and to assess the degree to which the participants have been motivated. Expression of attitudes, subjective opinion and even constructive criticism may prove valuable for evaluation.

It is very essential to evaluate the training programme to bring about improvements and this makes it more effective. This may be based on the comments and suggestions given by the trainees. In fact, a training programme is continuously evaluated by the participants any trainers alike. It is, therefore, sensible to clearly build into the programme the on going review which would help in identifying the gaps in training and better plan future programmes.

Evaluation of programme towards the end can at best be "reaction-oriented" and not "learner oriented". Therefore, evaluation should be done weekly, fortnightly or monthly in case of long-term programmes. Weekly evaluation is very useful in long-term training programmes.

On-going evaluation runs through the pro-grammes. It may be done daily, weekly, fortnightly or monthly depending upon the length of the training programme. This type of evaluation is more useful because participants could give feedback on topics already covered on the basis of which the remaining part of the programme could be modified.

The concurrent evaluation can be done in the following training situation.

(i) Each participant is asked to give his own views through a schedule questionnaire filled during or at the end of each course/session;

(ii) Each trainee is asked to give his/her views through a schedule or a questionnaire in writing at the end of each block or at the end of the whole course.

(iii) Discussion takes place between representatives of the trainees as well as the trainers: and

(iv) There is an open discussion on the assessment of the programme/course in the classroom and the teacher or a trainee takes notes.

Mid-course evaluation

Apart from evaluation of each period or session, there could be a mid-course evaluation if the curse is of longer duration. This will help in improving a training porgramme. The concurrent and internal evaluation may help in applying mid-course corrections of the curriculum, teaching methods, aids, organisation etc. Therefore, one has to evolve some procedures for concurrent evaluation of the progress towards specific training objectives. If the concurrent evaluation is under taken more frequently in the course of the programme and at regular intervals it tantamounts almost to the 'monitoring of programme' as the monitoring also aims at keeping the pace and direction. The final or terminal evaluation comes later to review its relevance the programme objectives the needs of the work, organisation and the job etc.

Concurrent evaluation can be carried in two ways:

i) by measuring the participants' progress towards the training objectives at a specific time.

ii) by providing in the syllabus for regular programme review sessions.

Evaluation of the progress is rooted in the set of objectives laid down for the training event or the block of events in the syllabus. At the expiry of the particular block the participants/trainees are expected to know these events.

Final terminal evaluation

Evaluation at the end of the course may not be very realistic in as much as the participants may not usually wish to say uncomplimentary or uncharitable things about the terms and/or the training agency. The trainees are generally overwhelmed with feelings of parting after living together for sometime due to the training opportunities provided by the agency. Therefore, such an evaluation may not yield good results. At best the feedback may help in bringing about marginal improvements in the future training programmes.

Course evaluation

End course evaluation is more likely to be trainer oriented such and evaluation tends to be based. The sentiments of participants would often get mixed up with objective facts. They may also forget certain aspects of training and may not be sure what exactly to say on the aspects. End course evaluation would prove useful in short term courses.

The trainer engages trainees before/after training through

- Letters, personal contact, telephone, conference and group conferences.
- Relating trainees to each other.
- Data-gathering questionnaire.

- Taped reporting.
- Involvement in planning next training session.
- Interim assignments or written job descriptions.
- Sharing of critical incidents.
- A problem census.
- Forecasting an image of trainee's potential one year hence.

Areas of evaluation

Evaluation of a training programme should include the following areas/ questions:

Contents

(a) To what extent the contents were relevant to the listed objectives?

(b) Were the contents given adequate coverage?

(c) Was the sequencing proper? Was there any overlapping and duplication?

Methodology

(a) To what extent the training methods used were useful and relevant to the contents?

(b) Whether a particular method went well with the contents or did it require a different method or a combination of different techniques?

Facilities

Were the infrastructural facilities like board and lodging, classrooms adequate and conducive to the learning process or inadequate and affected learning.

Group relations

Group relations/group dynamics should also form an area of evaluation. Evaluation should see whether the group relations were developed enough to promote homogeneous relations among participants or there was any need to use proper methods to develop such a relationship.

Resource persons

Resource persons are one of the important inputs of training. Therefore, feedback on the quality of resource persons also becomes important like where they well-informed? Did they possess necessary skills of communication?

Personal development

Course evaluation should include the area of personal development. The evaluation should see whether the trainees got any opportunities for personal development? If not, what were the inhibiting factors? Trainees could evaluate group relationship by observing to what extent the group was cooperative or what was the contribution of trainees to the course?

Process of evaluation

(i) At the end of the course, the trainees may forget some of the points if there is no regular/ concurrent evaluation, where opportunities are given to the trainees to express their views;

(ii) Experience shows that at the end of the course, the trainees sometimes become emotional and speak more of the positive aspects. On the other hand if they did not get good physical facilities, particularly boarding and lodging, stipend etc., they tend to be critical and the physical arrangements dominate. The contents covered and the methods used are forgotten.

(iii) At the final evaluation, the trainees may be asked to fill an assessment sheet. This should be analysed by the trainers and the results placed before the trainees at the concluding session of the course/programme.

(iv) There should be a system of asking the participants to express their views at the end of the course or at the concluding session;

(v) The views of some of the trainees sometimes are conditioned or influenced by the views expressed by those who are more vocal and dominate during the programme.

External evaluation

Some of the training centres are confident of their performance. At the same time they are keen that the training programme should be improved and strengthened further. They invite criticism of the training programme. Therefore, apart from concurrent, mid-course of internal evaluation they also go in for evaluation by an external agency or an expert who after consulting the trainees, the trainers, participating agencies and visiting field situation are able to give some very useful feed-back to the training institution. This information will be useful in improving the future training programme from various angles.

Post-training evaluation

After training, the participant goes back to his work situation. He is well equipped with new knowledge, new aptitudes and skills. His performance in the field/practical situations, depends upon how effectively he/she has been trained and the support he gets to meet the needs of working environments. An attempt is made to assess the impact of the training or the job performance of the trainees. The feedback may also help in bringing about necessary improvements in the job training.

Training assessment may be made by the training institution or by an outside agency. The post-course evaluation may be based on the following:

(a) Concurrent evaluation by the trainees.

(b) Concurrent evaluation by the trainers.

(c) Discussion at the plenary/concluding session.

(d) Evaluation sheets filled in by the trainees at the end of the course/programme.

The post-training evaluation is of two kinds—one which takes place immediately on the termination of the course and the other is which is conducted after the trainees have been placed in their field situation. In such evaluations, the usefulness or efficacy of the trainees in field situations is assessed.

Sometimes the letter received from the trainees may also add useful dimension to the final evaluation.

The trainer should have a balanced approach. He/she should be able to accept the failures and mistakes and the basic belief that there is always room for improvement. He/she should always try for further improvements in the training programme and should be able to assess the merits and demerits of the evaluation objectively.

Impact evaluation

A training programme as a whole can be ultimately evaluated by the performance and impact of ex-trainees after the training-perhaps only some years after wares in the case of training for development. The part played by a particular course or a series of inputs within a training programme can be evaluated by discovering how far it has contributed to the trainees' overall competence. Care should, however, be taken that there is not too big a time lapse between the training and evaluation lest the trainee should forget most of what he learnt during the training. At the same time it may be ensured that the trainee had sufficient time after training to test in the field situations the principles and techniques learnt during the training.

Retrospective evaluation is typical of an academic approach. For this approach continuing evaluation is more appropriate, especially because of sufficient flexibility in each course for adjustments to be made in content, methodology, inputs and timetable. More than that continuing evaluation is an integral part of the approach to training which we are using. It fits with an emphasis on the process of 'starting where people are,' and with a methodology which is 'experience-based, open-ended, individual and group-centered, and largely here-and-how'.

Evaluation at field level

The training institutions in their own interest should remain in touch with what happens to the trainees/ participants and the institutions nominating/deputing them after the trainees/participants go back and report for work. This is to be seem mainly to view that to what extent:

i) the training has helped the trainees perform their jobs better.

ii) the training institution has benefited form the trainee having rendered better service.

iii) feedback has helped the training institutions to improve:

   a) knowledge base,

   b) imparting of skills,

   c) use of methods,

   d) use of aids, and

   e) developing or improving the training infrastructure.

This could be done in a variety of ways:

i) The trainees should send a periodical report of field work with special reference to utilisation of the training skills, the knowledge they acquired etc. Through a well structured proforma.

ii) It could even be through an ordinary letter written by a trainee.

iii) One of the trainers occasionally visits the institution/ project to see the performance of the trainees in the field situation to see if and to what extent the training has helped him or created problems for him.

iv) The trainees should continue to get some king of information on a continued basis form the training institution such as a Newsletter, fresh guidelines on the programmes, as also literature on similarly run but successful projects else where.

v) Refresher courses which may be very useful not only to the trainees but also to the institution who organise job training: and

vi) Occasionally seminars, workshops, conferences may be arranged inviting also the trained persons to narrate some experiences of successes or otherwise.

Periodically, the training institutions should have a feedback as also the trainees assessment of the trainers which they had given before leaving the training centre in remodelling their training programmes form the point of view of contents, methods, aids etc. Or evaluation done after a lapse of time when the trainees have gone back to their jobs may yield lasting dividends:

The questionnaires seek to bring out the element of content of training, as also comment is in regard to the performance of the trainer. While it is accepted that the evaluation of such training vis-a-vis the trainers should logically begin with an appraisal of the programme needs, it also proves that once such programmes are approved, they should be continuously developed over a period of time. This is, of course, subject to the consideration that needs to be given during the initial phase to the evaluation of training itself, including such fact as the length of the training programme, the adequacy of instructions, the course-content and its impact on the principal objectives of the training etc.

However, the trainer should remember that the mid-course or ongoing evaluation does not replace final evaluation of the programme. The final evaluation should cover the entire programme-its objectives, contents, materials, methods, trainer's behaviour, living arrangements etc. evaluations should be learner oriented and not trainer oriented.

True evaluation of the course could be done at the field level on the basis of job performance of trained persons after they have worked at least for three months. Feedback on his/her performance could be got from the trainer himself, his colleagues, his juniors,, beneficiaries, supervisors and bosses.

Transfer of training to the field

An important ingredient of training is its utility in day-to-day life and work situations in particular. What is learnt at the training centre needs to be transferred to real life situations? Transfer of learning should be carefully planned because transfer does not take place automatically. In order to ensure effective transfer of learning to real life situation, the training programme must provide opportunity to plan this transfer. It is important that clear conscious and adequate attention is paid to transfer of learning. The transfer to training to the field follows certain steps. These steps are:

Consolidation of learning

A trainee should know that whatever he could learn should be applied to field situations. For this purpose, the entire learning during the course should be consolidated so that he would be in a position to apply it in his job behaviour as also enhance his knowledge, skills and performance. Knowledge gained during the course should not be alien form the job.

A trainee should have faith in himself to be able to transfer training to the field. He should be fully committed to it. This commitment and faith has to be developed in the trainee which can be further reinforced by the agency where he is working. If the trainee has the feeling or commitment to his work, it becomes easier for him to face all constraints he might have to face at the time of application of learning in a job situation.

A trainer should never ask the trainee to transplant his learning but should tell him to adopt it to the field.

Process of learning

Process of learning takes place at two levels; i.e. subconscious and conscious or at 'manifest' and 'latent' level. Most of our learning is processed at 'subconscious' or' latent level, which is not readily available for our reference. Keeping these levels in view a trainee must have an idea of the gaps in his performance before training and inputs he has received during the training programme. This could help him to transfer his learning into the field. Such a transfer is possible only when learning is thoroughly processed and consolidated on the basis of his past experience and present learning. The material provided by combination of past experiences and the "here-and-how" experiences generated during the programme would, if processed thoroughly, help to a great extent in the transferring of learning into the field.

Mobilizing support for transfer

By sharing learning experiences a trainee had from a training programme, with the colleagues, superiors and subordinates, can simplify the process of implementation of new ideas, knowledge and skills. The could also help him mobilize support from his fellow-beings as they would also become aware of his activities. Awareness raising is most aptly achieved through dialogue between the trainee and his colleagues, superiors, subordinates etc. It also entails critical examination of objective and subjective reality of work situations. Relevant and precise information and inputs can thus be disseminated. Sometimes, even the persons who are reluctant and act as disturbing elements may also support the individual trainee is his transfer of training into field.

Creating opportunities

Instead of waiting for opportunities, it is there responsibility of a trainee to create opportunities for transfer of his learning into the field. A systematic sharing of trainee's experience, knowledge and skill gained during the training programme with his fellow workers in his organisation is one of the surest ways of creating such an opportunity. This would help him to create a suitable environment which is a crucial condition for the utilization of learning into work situation.

Identification of supportive/resisting factors

Identification of supportive and resisting factors is very important so that the individual could plan properly and act accordingly. The trainee himself needs to be aware of his won self and sensitive to others' strength, needs and feelings in the organisation he is working for. He should have skills of working in cooperation with his colleagues, bosses and subordinates and a keen sense of observation in respect of individuals to recognise the supportive and resisting factors.

Follow-up of training

All training programmes must have a follow up component. The follow-up can be through visits, short meetings and news-letter. Follow up is useful both to participants as well as the trainer; the former gets assistance and support beyond the porgramme, the latter gets insight into the impact of the programme in local conditions.

Pitfalls in evaluation

Failures in evaluation can be attributed to inadequate planing, lack of objectivity, evaluation errors, improper interpretation of findings etc. poor systems of evaluation programmes do not provide firm data for improving and controlling the quality of a training programme.

Assessment of effectiveness

After a training programme has been devised and implemented we may test its effectiveness to decide whether

i) the training needs were correctly identified?

ii) the training programmes met those needs?

iii) the results obtained were commensurate with the cost?

iv) the same results could have been achieved more economically through some other strategy?

Maintenance of records

For the purpose of assessment, training records are to be maintained to provide both the personal records relating to the progress and potential of the people being trained and the data on which the effect of the programme as a whole can be judged. Measurement of progress should, as far as possible, be based on objective criteria, using, for example, attainment tests or similar measures, appropriate to the various levels of training. Trainer' reports and appraisals should usually be based on objective judgments. The opinion of the employing supervisor or manager on the quality of work done after formal training, will also be needed an should be called for. Where practicable, the application of simple statistical techniques and the use of control groups can help in measuring quantitatively the improvement that has taken place. If the training has succeeded in its objectives, it will be possible to judge whether the objectives were sound by comparing the new job performance with the assessed need. Since the aim of training is improved performance on the job, measure of performance must be made not only at the a conclusion of the training programme but also later.

Cost effectiveness

Some assessment of the cost effectiveness of training should also be attempted, for its economic justification . This should be done in collaboration with the agencies to help to work out means of comparing the cost of training and its effectiveness. Assessing the cost of training off the job, whether it is carried out within an agency or externally, is not difficult; on the job training costs are not so easily identified but if the true costs of training are to be assessed, an attempt can be made by identifying the elements which make up the cost of training.

Assessing the cost effectiveness of training is practicable in cases where specific skills or techniques have been taught and are immediately put to use. These measures of efficiency will also apply to skill training. Valuations thus made may then be set against the cost of training, assessed by cost analysis techniques. There are some forms of training which are required on both human and economic grounds, but they should still be subject to analysis to establish the cost.

Methods of measuring participant's progress are:

i) Observations.

ii) Simple tools for cross-checks.

iii) Check list to ensue observance of different aspects of training.

iv) Rating scales which allow measurement of opinion and feeling.

v) Content analysis of written and spoken words serves to measure understanding.

vi) Analysis of simulation sessions indicates the degree of skills with which the participants handle situations.

Constraints of evaluation

Despite the fact that an emphasis is now being laid on the importance of evaluation of training, there are built-in constraints in this process. Some of these are:

i) Trainee is in a psychological mood to leave.

ii) He may be mindful of the problems he is going to face when be goes back home to the same background from which he had come.

iii) Sometimes reactions of the participants may be influenced by other non-academic considerations such as facilities provided.

iv) Since it is time for the group to part, they may become emotional.

v) There are various complex factors the interaction of which complicates the process further.

vi) There is no foolproof and objective system or tools of evaluation.

The trainers and evaluators have, therefore, to construct their evaluation procedure and tools very carefully and objectively.

Drawbacks of the training

The training could be a failure due to the following factors:

(i) Unrealistic goals

(ii) Input overloads

(iii) Alienation of participants

(iv) Linkage failures

One of the methods for helping the trainees in the posts training period, i.e. while they are on the job is to encourage trainees to refer back their problems, which however, could be done only in consultation with the authorities of the implementing agency organisation.

Problems of training

The training exercises/effort may suffer due to the absence of:

(i) a philosophy or policy for training

(ii) proper planning of the training

(iii) fully qualified, experienced and oriented trainers

(iv) facilities for trainer's training

(v) poor budgetary allocations for training

(vi) flexibility

(vii) action-research on training

(viii) field exposure and staff development

(ix) adequate incentives to the trainers

(x) general apathy towards training

(xi) proper physical infrastructure.

(xii) proper arrangements for evaluation of the training programme.

8

Establishing Training Needs

One of the most important steps in the training process is the establishment of the training needs. In using this term we are implying that there are weaknesses somewhere in the system which demand strengthening by means of training in some form or other. It is common to define a training needs as the gap which exists between the true requirements of a given job and the present capabilities of the incumbent. However, we must not confine our definition solely to the individual, although in the last analysis the satisfaction of needs will have to be carried out through individuals, The organization is seen to have needs when it recognizes that it is not geared to meeting the objective which it sets itself. In other words, when setting its targets it cannot make the assumption that the resources already available will be suitable or adequate. It therefore has to examine any short comings and make suitable provision in its plans for eliminating them. This involves among other things, establishing whether the organization structure and capability are right to meet the challenges of the future and identifying the needs which arise in the various functions or occupations throughout the business. Finally, individual needs will become evident when employees carrying out those functions are found not to be fully equipped, in terms of knowledge, skills or attitudes, to meet the requirements of their jobs.

In order to be able to measure the gap which has to be closed by means of training, it is therefore necessary to follow a three-stage procedure. We need to as certain, in some detail:

- the desired performance of the organization and its shortfalls in meeting its objectives due to training deficiencies
- the training needed in each occupation to enable that function to be carried out comprehensively and
- the expected contribution and present capability of each member fop the workforce.

It has already been indicted that the overall training needs in an organization will be highlighted by the business plans which indicate what the concern's activities are expected to be over the period of the plan. Corporate plans may be for any period from a few months to five or even ten years. It is however, most common for organizations to produce short-term plans for periods of one year and long term plans for periods of four or five years.

Let us suppose that the 1985 short-term corporate plan of a manufacturing plant, which is part of a large group, includes the following objectives:

- to complete development of product B by 14 December 1984. This models to supercede product A. Pre-production models to be available by 18 February 1985. Commence production 4 March 1985. Output target 500 units/ month for the first two months, there after 1000 units/month. Total output for 1985 9000 units; 1986 12,000 units
- to phase out product A by 3 May 1985. Forecast monthly requirements in 1985: January 840; February 730; March 380; April 420
- to introduce incentive bonus scheme on product B

line with effect from 4 March 1985

- to install tow model PX 870 word processors in Sales Department by28 January 1985
- to adopt the group financial reporting systems by 1 January 1986.

This information, although limited, provides the training department with some clues about future training needs, which may be summarized as follows:

1. It is assumed that production workers will not have been sitting around idle, and that their numbers will be in line with the needs of production in January and February 1985. This means that since the level of output is expected to rise considerable from March onwards, more production workers will be required unless productivity can be dramatically improved! The numbers will be revealed in the manpower plan and there will be two obvious training needs. First, the existing workforce will have to be re-trained on the new model and second, the new intake will require introduction and job training. If the new model is very different from the old, the supervisors may also need familiarization with the revised requirements.
2. An incentive scheme should not be introduced with out adequate communication with the workforce. If management wishes it to work, the people involved must accept it and fully understand it. Thus training is again indicted for the operatives, the supervisors and possibly the managers. Members of the wages/ salaries department will also have to be familiarized with the scheme.
3. The installation of equipment which will change working practices in a department will inevitably give rise to the need for training those affected. The

employees in the sales department who will use the word processors will have to be instructed in their operation.

4. Changing the financial reporting system i an establishment by directive from head office can have far-reaching implications. Not only does the financial department itself have to be initiated in the revised procedures and possible in a new philosophy, but the managers and supervisors who are parties to implementing the system will like wise require training in carrying out the new requirements. Failure to prepare both specialists and managers to operate modifies reporting systems in this way can cause considerable confusion an make the transition from old to new much more difficult than it needs to be.

The findings at this stage are vague. They really only tell us that some training will have to be done. Although numbers of potential trainees will be available from the manpower plan, the magnitude of the task is not evident since we have not yet established how much new knowledge or skill has to be acquired by them. The first step, then, is to analyses the new requirements.

Job analysis is the term used to describe a process which involves the analysis of a job into its component parts or tasks to provide the data required for a variety of purposes. These include recruitment, management development, developing organizational and wage structures, improving job methods and safety and, of course, establishing training needs. The general principles of job analysis are applicable to all situations, whether in the factory, the office, maintenance of servicing departments both in plant and in the field, in fact anywhere where work is being done. It tends, however, to be associated in people's minds more with manual and craft jobs and possibly clerical work, than with management, supervision or other professional areas. This arises from the fact that manual jobs generally involve more easily definable processes or activities and consequently they would appear to be more suitable areas in which to use analytical methods. Management and professional work is less clear cut and attempts to analyse such jobs are likely to meet with greater opposition from the people concerned, who feel that much of their work is empiric and not susceptible to detailed examination. Nevertheless, the analysis of such work can pay dividends in, among other things, improving the management of time and thus helping to optimize managerial performance. It is a common criticism of managers in the 1980s that they spend unnecessarily long hours at work and need to learn to manage their time more effectively.

In the course of carrying out a job analysis, a job description or a job specification is prepared. The distinction between these terms is that a job specification states what a job should be whilst a job description sets out what it actually is, taking into account the specific knowledge and skills the job-holder brings to it. Clearly when someone is recruited to a job, he seldom matches the job specification precisely and often it is necessary to modify the duties and responsibilities to make use of the skills and knowledge that the newcomer can bring to the position. In some instances, the job descriptions of other people in the department may well be modified in order to accommodate the new arrival and to optimize departmental performance. Note that this does not mean that either of these documents tells us how effectively the job is performed by the job-holder. That is taken care of in the performance review or by some other means of assessment.

It will thus be seen that where we are examining a newly

created job, we produce a specification based on what we think the job should look like. Where the position is already occupied by an employee, it is possible, with the benefit of the experience of the job-holder, to write a job description setting out precisely what it entails. In either case the document should normally cover:

- the scope and purpose of the job and its objectives
- the work performed in the job: the detailed functions/duties and whether operational, supervisory, or managerial etc.
- the responsibility for (a) resources, quantified where possible under the six M's: manpower, machines, materials, methods, money and minutes, and stating clearly where accountable; (b) policy decisions, whether individually or through committees
- the organizational relationships, i.e. position in the hierarchy, cross-functional interfaces
- the training and experience needed
- the working conditions, eg (a) location; (b) nature of work activity; (c) hours of work; (d) whether member of a group; (e) health/safety risks
- the pay scale and conditions of service
- the opportunities for advancement within the organization.

To produce such a document we therefore need to know a good deal about the job and where it fits into the general scheme of things. If the post is deemed to be necessary to the future of the organization, it should not be too difficult to define its purpose. No job should exist without a clear statement of its scope and intent and the objectives the job-holder is expected to achieve. For example, the objectives of a personnel manager may be:

- to promote and maintain sound industrial relations practice throughout the organization
- to recruit employees at all levels below first line management in sufficient numbers and of acceptable standard to meet the needs of the manpower plan
- to contribute to the formulation of company personnel policies and agreements and to ensure their effective implementation
- to establish the training needs of employees are all levels and to take the necessary steps to se that these need are satisfied
- to provide a welfare service to employees at all levels and to implement health and safety policies.

Tabulating the work performed in the job may be more difficult. We can readily establish whether it is a managerial, supervisory, specialist or operational job but ascertaining the detailed functions to be performed requires analysis and may have to be approached indifferent ways depending on the job. One thing is certain. The process entails the collection and examination of a good deal of data, some of which will be considered appropriate for inclusion in the job analysis and some of which will be rejected. Where the job is already being carried out, one what in which such data can be accumulated is by discussing it with the job-holder. He should be in possession of as much information as any one and often he will be able to offer facts, gleaned form experience, which no one else knows about. Off course, approaching the employee for such a purpose requires care. He needs to be put at his ease and reassured as to the reasons for the exercise. He must not see it as putting him under any threat, for example of being moved, or worse, of losing his job altogether. Once such worries are dispelled, he will normally be very happy to talk about his job.

It is not enough merely to ask the job-holder what he does. If we have training needs in mind we shall want to know how he does his job and why he does it i a particular way. We may discover that he has got into the habit of employing inefficient work methods. This may point to the need for a closer examination of the whole job by the work study department, who will establish by scientific means the most suitable methods to be used in carrying out the job.

TWI job breakdown

A job involving a number of operations proceses or tasks may have to be broken down in to manageable parts. There are several ways in which this may be done. Perhaps the most simple of these is the. Training Within Industry breakdown for job instruction. Although the TWI courses run by the Manpower services Commission were phased out in May 1984, the method of breakdown used has stood the test of time and is still found to be helpful in the absence of anything more sophisticated. The trainer is recommended to work through the job once to identify stages or units which he believes contain no more than the average learner is able to master at a time. He then goes through the job a second time and looks for essential factors in doing it properly.

These are called key points and are factors:

- that may make the job easier to give special guidance on carrying it out
- that may have safety implications, or
- that may affect the quality of the finished work.

Task analysis

Task analysis is another method of breaking down a job. This is defined in the Department of Employment's Glossary of Training Terms as 'a systematic analysis of the behaviour required to carry out a task with a view to identifying areas of difficulty and the appropriate training techniques and learning aids necessary for successful instruction.' The tasks in a job are listed and each one is then analysed in order to evaluate its importance and the degree of difficulty that may be experienced. The means of dealing with the task in training terms are then identified. By way of a simple example, fig. shows part of a task analysis of the job of a scales assistant in a retail shop.

Faults analysis

Where the incidence of errors of faults in a job can be fairly high, the faults analysis method can be useful. The reasons for and consequences of the faults or errors are assessed and the necessary training action planned. An example of the use of this techniques is as follows:

A service engineer has an adequate technical knowledge to under stand the basic operation of all the products he has had no practical experience of trouble-shooting on Unit X. This unit has a fault pattern which is fairly consistent, eg 80 per cent of faults are failure of component Y resulting in certain symptoms and the other 20 per cent are also fairly predictable. The need is quite obvious here. He does not have to be acquainted with the detailed operation of the unit, but does require a be acquainted with the detailed operation of the unit, but does require a run-down no the most frequently recurring faults. Just how much information has to be imparted depends upon his existing knowledge and expertise.

Another example of the use of the faults analysis approach is with the job of a conference organizer.

It is relatively easy to produce a checklist of the basic activities and duties of such a person , but the acid test of his or her success comes when things go wrong and have to be dealt, with promptly to avoid a disaster. A list of such eventualities can be made. For example, the failure of a speaker to arrive at the appointed time, the breakdown of a visual aid during a presentation, the out break of fire in the building, hiccups in the catering services ordered, and so on. Being forewarned of the most common critical incidents in this person's job, it is possible to provide suitable training to enable them to be dealt with effectively should they arise.

Skills analysis

Perhaps the most common method of analysing the skills required in work of a non-supervisory nature in industry or commerce is that known simply as skills analysis. The main requirements of this method are that it should be systematic and that it should provide enough information to enable a suitable training programme to be designed. It may be used for simple or complex jobs.

This breakdown does not give detailed information on how to use the shredding machine. This would have to be provided in the training programme developed form the skills analysis.

In more complicated jobs it may be necessary to incorporate an ergonomic study of the job. Ergonomics, as defined by Professor W T Singleton in his Introduction to Ergonomics, is 'the technology of work design', and is 'based on the human biological sciences: anatomy, physiology and psychology. In general terms, anatomy is concerned with the structure of the body and psychology is concerned with behaviour. Thus in analysing a job which involves more complex skills, we may have to concern ourselves with:

- matching the working conditions to the physical build of the employee

- the precise movement patterns of the limbs used in carrying out work manoeuvres
- the physiological and psychological effects of environmental conditions such as heat, light, dirt, noise, vibration
- the employee's motivation and attitude towards the job.

In general, such a detailed scientific analysis of a job requires a specialist who may be found in the internal work study department or among the ranks of independent consultants.

Since it is not possible to do justice to the subject of ergonomics in a few paragraphs, a description of its various aspects will not be attempted here. Training staff who wish to explore the topic in detail are recommended to read Singleton's book mentioned above.

Returning to the employee's job description, we have examined the objectives of the job and analysed the work performed in it by breaking it down into its various duties and functions. A further part of the job analysis is the establishment of responsibilities for resources and policies. The manager or supervisor who is on the next rung up in the hierarchy will usually be most concerned with settling his subordinate's responsibilities. Being accountable for the total operation of his department, he will allocate responsibilities by delegation and the extent of that delegation will depend on a number of factors, including the training which he has given his staff to fit them for duties at a higher level. Unhappily, this is not the average manager's strong point. He often avoids delegation because of his fear of the subordinate being unable to cope, failing to carry out the job satisfactorily and thus bringing the manager himself into disrepute. Another fear is that if the subordinate knows too much the manager feels that his own job may be under threat. The first situation is less likely to arise if the employee is a suitable person to take on more responsibility, is given the necessary training and help to prepare him for it and is monitored periodically without his feeling that he is being closely supervised. The second fear, whilst being shortsighted, is understandable, but it is fair to say that no organization worthy of the name is going to sack its manages if they show the competence that is expected of them in developing their subordinates to the full.

Assuming, then, that the manager is carrying out his own responsibilities adequately, he will be able to establish those of his subordinates with little difficulty. He will know what the organizational structure of his department is and thus how many other employees report to each of his immediate subordinates. Similarly, the responsibility for the other resources such as materials and equipment will be clearly defined. What may not be so evident is the policy-making machinery. Whilst this should be quite clear in the interests of avoiding misunderstandings, it very often emerges as an ad-hoc activity, with disastrous results. In the absence of any clearly understood policies, people will make their own. This may work quite well for a long time if the quality of the personnel is high, but sooner or later something will go wrong. The most likely problem will be that ad-hoc policy decisions will be in consistent and this can often cause reactions which are worse than those from decisions which are downright bad. Training managers would be wise to stress the importance of the responsibilities for policy decisions being clearly defined in job descriptions, and the training needs in this area should be carefully explored. Some employees have a group responsibility for certain aspects of policy decision-making through the medium of committees or working parties. Many attend such meeting without knowing precisely what their obligation are. Shared responsibilities become diluted respon-sibilities one's share of the burden. Most people who are in this situation would benefit from some training in obtaining optimum results from committees.

The organizational relationships of the individual will be reasonably easy to establish. He will have contacts with other departments in the organization, some on a regular basis, others infrequently. The interface between those departments and his own has to be managed in the best interests of furthering his objectives. Frequently personal factors affect this, He may get on very well with some and find others difficult to handle. If this is so, the cause of difficulty has to analysed and suitable steps taken to deal with it.

Listing the important working conditions in the job description should not present too many problems. Most of them could be the source of training needs, physical working arrangements, eg where the job is a sedentary one, may create difficulties of and ergonomic nature. Shift-working may prove unsuitable for some employees because it is out to phase with their normal metabolism. Flexitime may cause problems in terms of getting the work done at times convenient to the business. If the employee works as a relatively isolated individual, he may experience problems of integrating his work with that of other parts of the organization. If he is part of a working group, there could be interpersonal difficulties. There are, of course, health and safety risks in all jobs to a greater or lesser degree. It is important that every employee knows what the hazards are in his particular situation and what he can do to avoid them. All such problems can come to light by exploring the areas covered by the job description and can, of course, highlight a number of training needs. This list is by no means exhaustive.

Performance review, whether used as part of a management development scheme or not, is an effective means of establishing training needs, provided those carrying out the review are competent to recognize those needs when subordinates do not meet their targets. If we assume that this condition is fulfilled, the following example will illustrate how training needs might be identified at such a meeting. The dialogue is between a training manager, Peter, and one of his subordinate trainers, Clive in a large group of companies.

Peter : Morning, Clive. It's nice to see you looking so bright and cheerful on a Monday morning! How are things going?

Clive : Oh, pretty well, I think I have found the work most absorbing over the past few months. Hectic, but certainly rewarding in terms of job satisfaction. I only wish there were more hours in the day. I think I'm beginning to feel the pressure a bit.

Peter: Yes, there's so much to do, I think we're all feeling a bit pushed. Anyway, the purpose of this meeting is really to look at our performance over the past year and to make plans for the coming one. Are you happy with the way things have gone?

Clive: I've had my unpleasant moments, but on the whole I think things have worked out reasonably well. you've seen the figures and no doubt had quite a bit of feedback from elsewhere. What do you feel?

Peter: Well, certainly you have carried out all the jobs that we targeted for last year and I must congratulate you on your stamina and determination. On the whole, the feedback I have had has been very favourable bur there are on or two areas which I think we ought to have a look at. Have you any idea which they might be?

Clive: I've no doubt one of theme is them is the supervisor course I did in June...

Peter: What problems did you have with that?

Clive: It was odd. As you know, I've done quire a few of these now, and as far as I can tell they have all gone down pretty well. But with this one.... well, I just did not see m to be able to get onto the same wavelength as this group. We always expect things to be a little difficult at first when they are feeling their way and weighing things up, but these chaps never seemed to be at ease and at times I felt they were openly hostile.

Peter: How did they shoe this hostility, then?

Clive: In a number of ways. They criticized the exercises quite frequently, and a times they ganged up on me with the clear intention of opposing anything I said. I can't think what I did wrong.

Peter: Do you really believe you did anything wrong? Was this not just a case of the group mix? We know that no two groups are alike and we have to take the rough with the smooth. We can't win'em all, Clive.

Clive : But I have never experienced anything quite as serious as this before, Peter. I was at a loss to know what to do.

Peter: What did you try to do?

Clive: Well, I must say I tended to take the easy way

out by avoiding anything too controversial. Which of course was not over-helpful from a learning point of view. I really felt outnumbered and told them so, and they said 'Rubbish'!

Peter: Did these problems arise as much during recreation periods as during training sessions?

Clive: Come to think of it, no. They behaved quite differently off the job and I didn't feel so isolated. In fact, I played darts with them quite a bit.

Peter : It sounds as though there was not personal animosity, then?

Clive : No, I don't think so. They were perfectly friendly in the bar

Peter: Then, it seems to me you were up against a reaction to authority, and didn't know how to handle it.

Clive: That's exactly it. I remember now that they spent quite a bit of time both in syndicates and full-groups sessions knocking the management. It became almost an obsession with one group ...

Peter: ....and they saw you as representing the management

Clive: Yes, evidently, but how do I cope with this sort of thing in the future?

Peter: You may not have to. This may be a one-off. But if you feel nervous about the possibility of it recurring, I suggest we look for an advanced course on interpersonal relations and managing groups. Preferably one in which the consultants specialize in dealing with real problem brought by the participants. I'm not sure who would be the best people at the moment, but I'll make some enquiries and perhaps You'll do the same. We'll meet again at the same time next Monday and get it sorted out.

Clive : Thanks!

Peter: Now about the other problem...

In this example, a problem has been talked through and a training solution agreed upon. It may not necessarily but the right solution, because the assumptions made may not be correct. Nevertheless, there is a rationale for the identification of the problem and for its solution. Training needs can therefore arise in this way. It is more common, however, for needs identified in performance reviews to be more clear-cut. For example, if a target is easily quantifiable it is much easier to decide whether or not it has been met. If a salesman's target requires him to sell a given number of products in a given time, it will be obvious whether he has met it or not. It is important, however, to establish what factors may have prevented him from reaching his target. Some may be completely outside his control, for example, changes in the law affecting credit agreements or failure of the factory to deliver the goods on time, although he may have a limited influence on the latter. Where his failure arises from lack of knowledge or skill, or the factory to deliver the goods on time, although he may have a limited influence on the latter. Where his failure arises from lack of knowledge or skill, or from having the wrong attitude towards the company or his job, the need for training will show itself fairly readily. The value of performance review in establishing training needs lies in the fact that boss and subordinate arrive at conclusions jointly. This tends to remove the objection that ad hoc and arbitrary decisions are taken to send people for training. The needs emerge naturally from a regular process which is accepted as part of the day-to-day operation of the department.

The use of pre-testing is usually associated with selecting people for employment. The aim is to obtain guidance in ascertaining what kind of work a person is suitable for or whether or not he is suited to work of a particular kind. Aptitude tests cover clerical work, shorthand/ typing, mechanical comprehension, manual dexterity, languages, vision and artistic skill, technical attainment and there are also rests of personality characteristics. These tests, among others, may be used in selecting people for training. If it is possible to discover in advance whether or not an employee has the capacity for learning to do work of a particular kind, time and resources may be saved in selecting out those who are unsuitable. Several agencies produce catalogues of test materials available and most of them apply strict user qualification conditions. In other words, they insist on users of their test materials having undergone approved instruction in their use.

Psychological testing appears to have been in the doldrums for a number of years, of course, whose experience has confirmed their belief that such tests are a valuable aid to measuring characteristics which cannot be measured by other means. There are many more sceptics, however, who feel that psychological tests have to be treated with some reserve and cannot be relied upon to give them the answers they are seeking. They may be prepared to use them to confirm their findings by other methods, but when the tests conflict with those findings they prefer to back their own judgments.

There are sings that interest in occupation-related psychometric testing in particular for employee recruitment and performance review, is on the increase. One firm of consultants has developed a set of

Occupational Personality Questionnaires which, it is claimed. 'marks the first major British initiative in personality research for some years' and promises significant improvements on existing techniques.

Some special aspects

In this chapter so far we have considered the identification of training needs using the business and manpower plans performance reviews and certain forms of job analysis. In practice we may also find that we have to use out judgment and knowledge of the business to pinpoint training needs which are peculiar to particular jobs in the organization but which are not highlighted by the above means. We shall therefore be looking at some of these aspects in the following pages.

Managers

Since most of the blame for things going wrong in business is popularly laid at management's door, it may be though that managers are more in need of training than anyone else. It is often argued by the cynics that managers are not competent to carry out the heavy responsibilities entrusted to them. No doubt there is justification for such criticism in a small proportion of cases, but the vast majority of managers that the writer has encountered over a period of 26 years in industry have not been seriously lacking in knowledge or experience. They have been dedicated, energetic, hard-working people whose main deficiency, if any, has been the lack of ability to use their attributes to optimum effect. A good deal of the training required should therefore be centered around harnessing their knowledge and experience in the interests of achieving the improved performance of which they are capable.

It is not at all difficult to identify areas where managers would benefit from an update in the knowledge required in their particular jobs using the means already described. Often these requirements become clear to the manger himself when he finds that his decision making capacity is hampered by a lack of information about, for example, internal factors like how other departments in the business operate or external factors such as the national economy and government legislation. Training managers will also be aware of the inefficiencies and frustrations that arise from managers working as isolated individuals rather than as terms pursuing corporate goals.

The needs for training in interpersonal skills are not always easy to deal with. Few managers will readily concede that they have problems in handling people. Rather than admit that they lack the requisite skills, many will blame the society in which we live for difficulties experienced with people and resign themselves to being powerless to do anything about them. If this were true, why are some managements so much more successful in handling their workforces than other? This phenomenon presents the training manger with a challenge. He needs to be able to find a way to test the value of training in interpersonal skills within his organization. Where there may be opposition to tackling this head-on, there will be many opportunities to introduce behavioral approaches into other training programmes. Once managers have seen the value of dealing with their interpersonal problems in a certain way, they will be more receptive to the idea that training needs that they have dismissed in the past a as being non-existent are worth exploring in greater depth.

Training staff need to adopt a proactive as well as a reactive role in identifying training needs. It has been said previously that the responsibility for training in any department is that of the manger or supervisor. That is fine as long as he recognizes the needs when it exists, but many instances arise where something changes and the manager may not know about it. Examples of this are:

- government legislation, affecting the business or employment, which the manager does not monitor adequately

In such instances, managers rely on the training staff to keep than informed of what is happening and what the training implications for their departments may be. There are also countless situations where, because of the extensive contacts that the training department has throughout an organization, it becomes aware of needs of a general character which may not become apparent to individual managers. It is true to say that, however varied managers hobs may be there is a core of common training needs. That is, there are fundamental skills which every manager regardless of function, should posses. These include interviewing running meetings, delegation, coaching counselling instructional and presentation skills. When a need of this kind is identified by the training staff, a survey should be conducted in the organization to ascertain the demand before any internal training activity is set up.

Where the demand does not justify such an internal course, external facilities may have to be used to satisfy the limited needs. Fig.8 shows a design for a survey form suitable for use in medium to large organizations.

It is very common for specialists to be promoted within organizations into managerial jobs without any preparation for their new roles. The assumption is often made that, if they have proved themselves competent in the specialist role and have generally gained acceptance from the management and their work colleagues, they are suitably equipped to carry out the new responsibilities satisfactorily without training. Most organizations will have witnessed the calamities that this policy has brought about and yet the practice still persists. Even at the highest level the theory can be held that management is a sink or swim situation, if you do not succeed in swimming on your own you are unfit to be a manager. This is, in the writer's opinion, a fallacy. There are many competent specialists who would make competent managers if given the tools to do the job. Apparently, is seldom recognized that moving from a specialist job, which has rightly or wrongly been carried out in a parochial fashion, to a management one, entails a dramatic re-alignment of one's working objectives, one's attitudes and, frequently, one's allegiances. There has to be a re-orientation from carrying out one's limited role in a specialist function to approaching the new job within a total business framework. Every move in effect has to integrate with the business policy and the business objectives. Indeed, one is party, to a greater or lesser degree, to the formulation of that policy and those objectives. It follows, then, that a newly-appointed manager needs to know far more about the business and about its philosophy than was required in the specialist role that he has just relinquished. It is sometimes argues that those who aspire to high positions in organizations owe it to themselves and to those who promote them to learn what they need to know about business and about philosophy than was required in the specialist role that he just relinquished. It is sometimes argued that those who aspire to high position in organizations owe it to themselves and to those who promote them to learn what they need to know about business by self-development. Certainly this is a reasonable argument where a general knowledge of business management is concerned, but it is not a practicable in dealing with the idiosyncrasies of particular organizations. Training managers are therefore urged to recognize the need to provide adequate training in business orientation, specially tailored to the organization's needs, for those who assume managerial responsibilities, such responsibilities involve a thorough knowledge of the business plans strategy, policies, systems, and so on. Promoting someone into management also opens up a need to train him in those day-to-day skills which he is expected to have as a manager, such as the common needs skills already mentioned.

Supervisors

The role of the supervisor in an organization is a unique one. It is commonly said to be the most difficult of jobs, not because the duties are particularly arduous, necessarily, but because there tends to be a conflict of loyalties. Supervisors and themselves at one and the same time representing the interests of both the management and their workpeople, and this can lead to difficulties in carrying out their jobs effectively. It must be said, however, that some of the dilemmas that arise are not so much due to any organizational conflict as to the fact that the supervisors themselves are not always suitably trained to carry out their responsibilities. Here again, as with mangers, we can have a situation where someone is promoted into a supervisory job without adequate preparation. He has been working as a craftsman, operator, clerk, for example, in a department in which the supervisor's job becomes vacant. Because of his knowledge and experience of the work carried out by the department, it is assumed that he is the man for the job. There should, of course, be a substantial re-orientation around the new duties, but frequently the supervisor continues to involve himself in the technical or operational aspects of the department's work because that is what he knows most about and is most interested in and the supervisory duties which he should be carrying out are given scant supervisory duties which he should be carrying out are given scant attention. He cannot be wholly blamed for this because no one has told him precisely what is required in the job. He knows that he is expected him precisely what is required in the job. He knows that he is expected to precisely what is required in the job. He knows that he is expected to produce output, but when problems which are only indirectly related to output arise, he does not recognize them as coming within his remit. For example, he will refer all problems remotely concerned with personnel and training matters to the specialist department, when many of them should be dealt with by him personally. He will accept new employees from the personnel department without having interviewed them to assess their suitability for the work or to satisfy himself that they will integrate with his existing workforce. And yet he will still acknowledge responsibility for their performance.

Some years ago a medium sized manufacturing company called in some efficiency consultants with the object of improving organizational performance. They interviewed the supervisors and discovered that the amount of time they actually spent on supervision was minimal. They therefore told the supervisors what their jobs should really entail, and said that as from Monday morning they would no longer have to involve themselves directly in the practical work of the department or the keeping of records. In other words, their duties would be solely supervisory. Two of them said they would rather go back onto the shop floor!

The message for the training department is clear. Every individual who is promoted to a position of supervisory responsibility generates training needs, and every effort should be made to equip such employees with the skills to carry out their new responsibilities adequately. A good deal of care is needed in drafting job specifications and the utmost attention should be given to ensuring that supervisors understand precisely what their jobs entail.

It is easy to produce supervisors for training programmes which are unsuitable because the training needs have not been properly established. One should not fall into the trap of assuming that because they have responsibility for subordinates, their needs are similar to those of managers. A knowledge of the financial structure and reporting systems in the organization is important to managers for instance but does not have the same relevance for supervisors. The financial knowledge that they require is probably confined to costing systems to which they have a direct input. However much it may be deemed a good thing to introduce them to balance sheets and profit and loss accounts, it will not have the same importance for them and they are unlikely to be receptive, unless they are seeking promotion to managerial status.

Most organizations, whether in industry, commerce or the public sector, employ a substantial number of specialists, that is, people who devote their energies to particular functions or professions. They will be employed in finance and accountancy, engineering, science, drawing office, marketing sales, production, personnel, training, materials management, administration, architecture, survey-ing, planning, work study, maintenance, servicing.... and so on. Each group has a sphere of influence, each has its own jargon and each approaches its work in its own special way.

Frequently one group will not communicate with another simply because it does not understand the language used. An accountant may avoid going near an engineer for fear of being blinded with science. Ironically, the engineer may avoid contacting the accountant for the very same reason-financial jargon means nothing to him. There would therefore appear to be a substantial need to help specialists understand each other's language in the interests of their working together for the common good. Strangely, these needs seldom emerge from the systematic approaches described earlier in this chapter, partly because people do not see training as a means of overcoming the lack of communication between departments or individuals. Here , then , is an area in which the training manager can be proactive. Since everyone else claims to be unable to communicate with accountants, it is rewarding to start here. Accountants and non accountants alike will welcome the introduction of training programmes in finance for non accountants. It helps the non accounting specialists to ask accountants the right questions, and to be able to understand the answers It also helps to impress upon those specialists that the fault for lack of communication rests just as much on them as on the accountants. From there one can move on to engineering for non engineers, marketing for non- marketing specialists, and so on.

There is a common misconception that engineers and scientists do not make good managers. This stems from the fact that they are seen to be very much wrapped up in things as distinct from people. They are deeply involved in and committed to their technical activities and may not therefore see what is going on around them. This is no reason to assume that they will no make good managers if they choose to move into the management ranks. The important thing is to recognize that this is so and thus to ensure that the machinery is available to enable them to cross that bridge and to be suitably trained for the new position.

Many of the training needs that arise for specialists are to update them in their particular field. This is a serious problem for technical people because of rapid technological change. It is, however, just as necessary for people in other areas to keep abreast of developments in their own fields. The difficulty that training staffs have is how this can best be done. They have to rely very heavily on the ability of the specialists bosses to identify areas of development which are pertinent. One way in which assistance can be given is to ensure that access is obtained to publications which report important new developments. Larger organizations have their own libraries which simplify the problem to some extent.

Field service or installation and commissioning personnel pose particular problems in assessing performance and consequently in establishing training needs. They have considerable freedom in discharging their duties on remote sites and it is uneconomical and impracticable to provide supervision on the hob. Much of their work therefore has to be taken on trust, because in the absence of any feedback from the customer there is no way of knowing whether they have carried out the requirements of the job satisfactorily or not. This points to a need to ensure that the highest selection standards are used for this type of employee in the first place. Some organizations deal with the training sessions at which the participants are encouraged to discuss their experiences in the field in some detail. Special difficulties are brought out into the open and, where appropriate, training solutions sought. Feedback from customers can also be of value in some instances. An atmosphere of openness and trust between managers and their field staff has to be created in order to make it possible for help to be given when needed.

Office workers

For some years the Industrial Training Boards have

recommended training programmes for clerical workers which are just as detailed as those proposed and adopted for other workers. In spite of this, less attention seems to be given to the needs of office workers compared with, say craftsmen or operators. The explanation probably lies in the fact that clerical work is not seen as requiring any skills that cannot be easily picked up as you go along. This attitude is unfortunate, because it can lead to gross inefficiencies in offices which would not be tolerated on the factory floor. There is sometimes resentment among blue-collar workers that whilst they are subject to tight restrictions on their activities and are required to meet demanding targets with the utmost efficiency, the white-collar workers appear to be free to work at a leisurely pace, to be wasteful in their use of office materials and not to be closely monitored. Whether this is true or not in particular situations, there is little doubt the in general office workers deserve more training that they get. Training specialists know only too well that properly planned and well directed training can have valuable pay of in any area of business and the offices are no exception. In the present days of economic recession, departments which are seen to contribute to overheads as distinct form wealth creating activities are the first to suffer cutbacks when businesses run into difficulties. It is there fore important that those who remain to carry the burden with reduced resources should be helped to do so as efficiently as possible.

One difficult area in offices is secretarial work. No two so-called secretarial jobs are alike, because each reflects the attitude to the job of the executive for whom the secretary works. The result is that she can be anything from a competent personal assistant who virtually runs the executive's job for him to an underqualified typist who is only sitting there to boost his prestige. There is often a high turnover in secretarial staff due to the fact that competent women are not given the responsibilities that they are capable of carrying out, When having to replace employees who leave for this reason, personnel departments would do well to insist on an undertaking from the executive that it some one with true secretarial skills is appointed, her capabilities will be suitably applied in the job.

The basic secretarial skills, such as shorthand, typing, office routine, arranging appointments are usually learned a secretarial college or by day release or even in study at a further education establishment. The skills needed to carry out a particular job, as has been said, centre around the relationship that exists between the secretary and the executive for whom she works. There is therefore merit in carrying out off the job training in which both parties are involved. This helps to remove some of the misunderstandings which frequently arise in interpreting the requirements of the job. It also provides the opportunity for promoting the idea in the minds of the executives that a good secretary properly employed is an invaluable asset. The jobs of both executive and secretary would have to be analysed before such training could take place.

Craftsmen

Analysing the hob of a craftsman, whilst it may be quite complicated if more that one skill is involved, is not difficult. It is largely a question of the observation of what activities are actually carried out by a skilled employee. It is not surprising then that when the Industrial Training Boars came into being after the Industrial Training Acts 1973 and 1981 was passed this was the area in which they concentrated their initial efforts

Considerable help and guidance has been given by Training Boards in the analyses of training needs for craft apprentices in providing basic training programmes and also additional modules to enable craftmen to extend their range of skills. Comprehensive information may be obtained from the appropriate Board.

Operators

like those of craftsmen, the analysis of the jobs of operators is fairly straightforward, and the job analysis methods covered earlier in this chapter are appropriate. In the interests of enabling operators to reach experienced worker standard without too much delay, a scientific approach to the analysis is desirable. In other words, after observing a skilled operator carrying out the job, it is helpful to have the working methods analysed by the appropriate work study specialist to ensure that the most efficient methods for the particular activity are being used. As mentioned elsewhere, it is not unheard of for event the best operators to lapse into undesirable work practices and take short cuts which are not acceptable either form the point of view of efficiency or safety.

Graduates

When organizations employ graduates, it is with the expectation that they are acquiring employees with trained minds who will fairly quickly be able to take on responsible work in the business. Tow major mistakes are made repeatedly. First, it is sometimes thought that graduates require as much detailed training as other young people and second, there are those who short time which other people have taken many years of their lives to equip themselves for. In the first case, it is important to realize that their minds are geared to assimilating information quickly and it is asking for trouble to expect them to operate a machine on a repetitive process for a period of months when they have learned all they need to know about the process in a week. It is generally true to say that for the types of jobs that they will aspire to they only need to know about the process in a week. It is generally true to say that for the types of jobs that they will aspire to, they only need to have an appreciation of the various processes that to make up the end product. there is no requirement for them actually to acquire the skills needed to carry out those processes. In the second case, whilst they come to work imbued with the confidence that they can very quickly assume responsibility, it is quite unrealistic to expect this without making certain that they are suitably equipped for it. It is therefore imperative that when we analyse the job that we ultimately want a graduate to do, we take special care to see that he is given the opportunity to acquire all the knowledge and skill needed to carry out that job effectively. He will, of course, be capable of acquiring a good deal of such information himself, but that does not exempt the employer form providing a comprehensive programme and adequate facilities to satisfy the graduate's needs. It makes economic sense to capitalize on a substantial investment.

The question of age and its possible influence on the establishment of training needs has not so far been mentioned. It would be very convenient to be able to say that its effect is negligible and can therefore be ignored. In practice, however, it is not possible to treat all employees alike in such a wide age range as 15 to 65 year. There is a temptation to believe that what is good for a mature adult in his 30s is suitable for everyone, but this is not the case. At either end of the working life there are particular needs which require special consideration. The young person entering the world of work for the first time faces a major adjustment to a totally new environment. He has spent much of his life in the company of young people and has been almost wholly dependent on his parents and the staff of the educational establishment that he has been attending. He not only has to adjust to the idea that he is moving into a period of relatively independent adulthood but also that the situation that he finds himself in is quite different form anything he has encountered before. Most of his working colleagues are likely to be mature adults, the work he is given to do will be new to him the business environment itself will be strange and the new rules, regulations and routines may be a little difficult to come to terms with. The training specialist has to be sensitive to these difficulties, the magnitude of which will very with the individual, and must ensure that they are adequately catered for when establishing the training needs of young people. this not only calls for understanding on the part of the training staff themselves but also on the part of the managers and supervisors for whom the young employees will be working. It is in the latter relationships that things sometimes go wrong, due to prejudices about the younger generation and a lack of appreciation of what problems they are having to face when they first go out to work. Trainers can make useful contributions to the handling of such difficulties by suitable inputs on this subject in management and supervisory training programmes.

The needs of adults at the other end of the age scale are different, though no less important. they centre around reassurances about their capabilities and a realization on the part of managers, supervisors and trainers alike that learning in late adult life takes time and requires special understanding.

It is unfortunate that so much training is carried out without regard for the basic principle that a clearly defined need should be established before deciding what training should be done. It is embarrassing for training departments to be told by course participants that they did not know why they were sent on the course because they could not see how it would help them in their jobs. Public courses have tended to encourage managers to adopt the line of least resistance. When they see details of a course which looks as though it might be interesting, they either nominate themselves or a subordinate without attempting to find out precisely what it covers. they find out too late that it is quite unsuitable, their needs are not satisfied, the company suffers and the training department loses credibility for allowing it to happen. the importance of analysing the true needs cannot therefore be overstressed.

9

Training Plans

The following training plans are included in this Chapter for the information and guidelines of trainers:

(1) Identification of social problems.

(2) Understanding Leadership Principles.

(3) Facts about Population-Introduction to Fundamental Population Concepts.

(4) Techniques for Identification of 'At-risk' mothers and children. Assessment of Nutritional Status in the field.

(5) Causes of Diarrhoea and its Prevention.

(6) Common Feeding Practices, Food Facts and Fallacies Among the Vulnerable Groups.

(7) Introduction of Supplementary Foods in an Infant's Diet.

(8) Assessment of Nutritional Status by Weight and Midarm Circumference Measurement Criteria.

(9) Use of Waste Material for making/learning Teaching Aids for Pre-school Work

(10) Common Nutritional Deficiency Diseases and Their Management.

(11) Assessment of Nutritional Status of Children.

(12) Mother's Awareness and Participation in Pre-school Education.

Behavioral objectives

Social Welfare Assistants will be able to identify various social problems, both over or subtle, as portrayed in the play.

Audio-visual aids/materials

(1) A four-scene play with script in Malay language.

(2) Chalkboard

Methods/strategies

(1) A play, depicting a family with mounting problems, is presented. Trainees should be able to identify various problems arising form the conditions of the family.

(2) Seating position: trainees are seated in a U shape. The trainer's table is placed in front.

The drama is about a man living with his wife and two children. Although the husband works only as a contract labourer, he earns sufficiently to satisfy the modest needs of the family; the family lives harmoniously. As time goes on, economic demands begin to increase and the family is beset with more problems. The wife, who has little education and who performs the daily chores of the family tries to do whatever she can to enhance the harmony within the family. But things do not turn out as she expects. On the other hand, the husband who is perturbed by the increasing financial burden, resorts to a seemingly easy way out. Under the influence of bad company, he starts taking drugs which ultimately leads him to criminal activities.

Through a kind hearted but inquisitive neighbor, the wife comes to understand the husband's plight. The father's changed behaviour has its impact on the lives of his children. The frail daughter becomes sick. The son begins to show behavioral problems; he manifests disrespect for elders, becomes a truant. He takes to bad company and is on the verge of dilinquency.

The wife being tied to household chores knows little of the outside affairs, she has little knowledge of sources of help. The kindly neighbor who is knowledgeable about many affairs of the villagers comes in to suggest that she get help from the Social Welfare Department.

Trainer's evaluation

The result of the recall test conducted showed that one of the trainees could identify all the sixteen problems. Only five trainees could state seventy-five percent of the problems and four of them could state sixty percent of the problems respectively.

After discussion the trainer moved round in the group and asked them to restate the problems. It is seen that the majority of the trainees are able to understand the problems. They are able to relate the concepts to practical situations. They are also able to see the relationship between problem identification and diagnosis and also its relation to the treatment. Trainees are of the opinion that the play as an aid to teaching reinforces their understanding of concepts.

Comments

(1) Dramatisation is good for many situations and takes less time. It appeals to our senses of hearing, sight as well as our emotions.

(2) It is a break from the normal media of communication. It adds variety to our teaching techniques. However, there are some disadvantages.

(i) The non-seriousness of actors/actresses can divert the attention of the course participants.

(ii) They may treat the drama as a piece of entertainment.

(iii) It gives a break from the monotony of the lecture method.

(iv) In a training situation, where time is insufficient, dramatisation is unsuitable.

Training session plan 2

Agency	:	Ministry of Culture, Youth and Sports,
	:	Malaysia
Trainer	:	Abdul Manaf Ibrahim
Topic	:	Understanding Leadership Principles

Behavioural objectives

At the end of the lesson the trainees will be able:

(1) to enumerate leadership principles such as the need for a leader, the role of a leader, group interaction, individual task and function in group achievement.

(2) to make and use the puzzle game in leadership training.

Trainer-learner activities

What the trainer does	*What the learners do*
(A) Members of the training team act out the play.	Watch the play.
(B) When the play ends the trainer asks the trainees to list the problems they perceived in fifteen minutes.	Trainees list the problems.

He asks the trainees to cite from their lists the problems they have identified. The trainer observes the pattern of presentation and asks the trainees to evaluate these.	Individual trainees cite the problems they have listed.
The trainer uses a chalkboard to reinforce the points.	Trainees evaluate these through discussion.
The trainer observes that out of sixteen problems presented in the play, the trainees pick out only a few; the trainer stimulates focus on other problems such as feeling s of hopelessness, insecurity, and rejection.	Trainees discuss the other problems.
(C) The trainer asks the trainees to relate their understanding of the problems to some of their practical experiences in the field.	The trainees cite examples, such as, the feeling of clients over the loss of their loved ones, and the feeling of a child who has to share the parents love over the arrival of another baby who gets more attention from them.
The trainer asks for opinions on the problems observed.	Trainees listen.
(D) The trainer relates the identified problems to their diagnosis and treatment.	The trainees point out that the economic problems have aggravated other problems; the daughter becomes sick because she loves the father and is very attached to his and now that he has deserted the family, she feels rejected. She is not able to fully understand the things that are happening within the family.
The trainer gives an example; the father deserts the family; the wife is left to fend for herself and the two children;she is faced with financial problems and	

has to get some assistance in order to relieve some of her problems. The trainer points out that the problems as presented by the person may not necessarily be those problems which are seen by the worker. The trainer asks the trainees to demonstrate this aspect from their practical field experience.	The trainees relate their practical experience.

Target group

(1) Active members of a youth organisation holding responsible positions in the organisation.

(2) Both males and females aged 18 to 30 years.

Number of trainees: Not more than 30 Training Time: 2 Hrs.

Audio-visual aids/materials

(1) Newspaper cuttings (125 pieces)

(2) Chalkboard

(3) Handouts

Methods/ Strategies to be used

(1) Participatory approach

(2) Group discussion

(3) Jigsaw puzzle game

(4) A summary and synthesis at the end of the lesson.

Summary of content

(1) Preparation of material

(a) Collect five sheets of used newspapers or periodicals with various headings or columns such as sports, world news, local events, entertainment, share market, etc.

(b) Using a pair of scissors, cut out twenty five different pieces from each sheet. Each piece is then pasted on used hard paper of cards of the same colour. The purpose is that the material can be utilized again.

(c) All the cuttings are placed on a table in the centre.

(2) Group activities

(a) The participants/trainees are divided into five groups.

(b) Each group is provided with a table. Try to arrange all the tables in a circle.

(c) Only one minute is given to each group representative to pick up any twenty-five pieces of the cuttings.

(d) The groups are instructed to make a complete page of a newspaper/ periodical out of the cuttings. The group which completes it first can be declared the winner. The other groups must also complete their tasks.

(3) Rules of the game

(a) Verbal communication among members or between members of different groups in prohibited.

(b) On their own initiative, a participant/trainee from any group can give away the cuttings not required, to the other groups. Taking any cutting without the consent of the group concerned.

(c) Each cutting must be given to any member of the group concerned.

(d) Any group which completes its tasks can surrender the remaining cuttings to the other groups.

Trainer-learner activities

Trainer's evaluation

(1) The trainees found that the game was very interesting.

(2) There was self awareness regarding groups interaction and individual functions as a member of the group.

(3) This game is time consuming, It is suggested that music can be added during the playing of the game proper.

Training session plan 3

Agency : National Family Planning Board, Malaysia

Trainer : Khoo Swee Kheng

Topic : Facts About Population-Introduction to Fundamental Population Concepts.

Behavioral objective: To expose the trainees to fundamental population concepts, so that they can train their subordinates to motivate more effectively the community in family planning.

Target audience: Senior para-medical personnel.

Educational qualification: Their general educational qualification is of school certificate level and state registered nurse.

No. of trainees: 30 Training time: Approx. 11-12 hours

Audio-visual aids/materials

(1) Chart " The New Salary Scheme"

(2) Workbook " Fundamental Population Concepts"

(3) Stencils—Correction Sheet.

Training methods/strategy: Group work Discussion

(1) The trainer promotes two-way communication and constant feedback through the use of simple problems which the trainers must answer in their group.

(2) There is personal involvement because each participant must personally find solution to simple problems.

(3) The theoretical and technical nature of a topic such as population growth is presented to the trainee through practical examples which makes the material easier to comprehend.

The use of this technique to presents a departure from the traditional lecture method and as such is itself an innovation in this area of training. Trainees find out facts about population by themselves and prove them through active group participation.

What the trainer does	*What the learners do*
(A) Request the participants to divide themselves into five groups.	The participants form their own groups.
(B) Instructions regarding the groups' tasks and the rules of the game are given.	The participants listen.
(C) Each group is asked to have its own discussions relating to the playing of the game.	Group discussions are held for five minutes.

(D) Representatives from each group are asked to pick twenty-five cuttings from the central table within one minute.	Each member of the group does his own task.
(E) Instructions to start the game is given,	Each member of the group does his own task.
(F) At the end of the game the trainer instructs the trainees to have group discussions regarding the experiences gained during the playing of the game,	The trainees form their own groups and discuss their experiences.
(G) The trainer then instructs the trainees to from a big group for a panel discussion.	The trainees form the groups and each shares his experiences by using the chalkboard.
The trainer encourages the trainess to reach to the experiences gained and summarise the knowledge gained.	Some trainees discuss the following and make moves on the chalkboard: (1) The difficulty they faced during the interaction because of the non-verbal communication. (2) The importance of appointing a group leader with the specific task of coordinating the work of the group. (3) Satisfactory interaction and cooperation among group members. (4) Interaction between groups was not very satisfactory because each group was emotionally involved in their own goal achievement. (5) The elements of jealousy and selfishness hindered the interaction.
(H) The trainer examplains how the game could be utilised in group interaction. (Handouts on how to	

	(6) The majority of the trainees became aware of their own weaknesses.
prepare the material are given.)	The trainees receive the handouts and answer some questions for clarification regarding the rules of the game.
(1) Evaluation: What benefits did you gain during the session?	Samples of the game materials are done as group activities. The trainees answer the question.

Summary of contents

(a) Describe the characteristics of geometric and arithmetic growth.

(b) Project population size based upon certain different growth assumptions using a simplified project model;

(c) Calculate the number of years for a population to double;

(d) Compare population growth with food production and discuss the implications:

(e) Discuss the amount of time it takes for a population to stabilise.

Trainer-learner activities

Trainer's Evaluation: Assessment of the performance of trainees by comparison with answer sheet.

Training session plan 4

Topic : Techniques for identification of 'at-risk' mothers and children. Assessment of Nutritional status in the field.

Behavioural objectives

Trainees will be able to:

(i) Know who are the 'at-risk' mothers and children.

(ii) Understand the principle of assessing the nutritional status in field by

- weight for age method
- mid-arm Circumference method.

Training time	:	1 hour 10 minutes.
Number of trainees	:	30
Trainees	:	The child development workers.
Seating arrangement	:	The trainees were seated in the normal classroom pattern.
Audio visual aids/ materials	:	Chalk and Black board.
Method/ strategies	:	Lecture

Teaching process

Time	*What the trainer does*
25 minutes	The trainer is introduced by the faculty member who also introduces the topic to the participants.
25 minutes	The trainer divides the topic into two parts and takes up the part who are the 'at risk' mothers and children; and the assessment of nutritional status. He lists 'at risk' children. Explaining each category, while discussing

	risk arising out of tetanus, a question asked what material is inclined in the Dai Kit. The answer is supplemented by the trainer. The second part of the topic-Assessment of nutritional status is taken up. The assessment is discussed at the following stages: (i) Community assessment

What the trainer does	*What the learners do*
(A) Divides the trainees in to five small groups.	The trainees group themselves.
(B) Informs them that we are going to spend some time talking about how population grows. Before that, we would like to talk about another kind of growth. There are two salary schemes being proposed. Explains each scheme. Repeats the description of each scheme if necessary. Instructs each participant to decide which scheme he/she wants.	Each person in each group chooses one of the two schemes, starting with the nearest trainee and going around the room.
(C) After each trainee has picked one scheme, the trainer hands out one chart- "The New Salary	Group works together to in the chart.

Scheme" -to each small group. Instructs group members to complete the chart together.	Ask questions if necessary.
(D) While the trainees are filling in their charts, the trainer circulates among the groups to answer any questions and to provide guidance.	Check calculations with this handout.
(E) When each group thinks it has correctly filled out the chart, the trainer gives each member of the group one copy of the corrected handout.	Answer which scheme was the better scheme, i.e, the new salary scheme, and why they completed this exercise, i.e, population growth is similar to the new salary scheme growth.
(F) After all groups have corrected their chart, the trainer talks to the entire group and asks them why they think they completed this exercise. Summarises the major points. Opens the floor for questions.	Choose a partner to work with.
(G) Collects all charts.	Proceed to work together in in pairs.
(H) After all questions have been answered, the trainer asks each group to choose a partner for the next section of the exercise.	Use this book to check the answer of the other sections they have finished.
(I) The trainee gives each pair one "fundamental population Concepts Workbook" and instructs the group on the use of the workbook.	Ask questions if necessary. Work as a group to complete this sheet.

Trainer activity	Trainee response
(J) The trainer also gives one copy of the "work-book Answer Sheet" to each group.	Each group corrects its won answers and makes the necessary modifications.
(K) The trainer moves among the trainees to make sure that each group correctly understands the assignment. He is available for questions/ advice.	The trainees spontaneously come up with most of these points. Ask additional questions, if any.
(L) After each small group has completed its workbook, the trainer instructs to complete the Summary sheet.	
(M) After the small group thinks, it has the correct answers to the summary worksheet, the trainer gives each trainee one copy of the answer sheet.	
(N) After all small groups have finished filling their workbooks and summary sheets, the trainer reviews the major points covered during the sessions. Open the floor for questions.	

	(ii) Family assessment (iii) Individual assessment (iv) These were written on the board.
20 minutes	The nutritional status assessment of a child by weight-height and mid-arm circumference is explained. Significance of

	the growth chart is explained. It is stressed that it was the well being and energy of the child, which reflected the nutritional status. The trainer invites questions form the trainees.	*What the trainees do* The trainees listen.
10 minutes	It is clarified that taking height would be an additional measurement to make as weight is a good and sensitive measure. The trainer answers the question by explaining how a local events calendar is prepared and how by interviewing the mother, the age can be found out. Once the programme gets under way the child care worker would know about the babies born in the village and so their exact age would be known.	Once of the participants answer the question. The trainees take down notes.

Observations and comments

(1) The lecture method used for the session was not only appropriate but also effective, since the objective of the session was to make the trainees know the 'at-risk' mothers and children. As each category was being introduced, it was written on the board, The whole list of 'at-risk' mothers and children was therefore, in front of the trainees, by the end of the session.

(2) For the assessment of nutritional status, principles of weighing and measuring mid-arm circumference were briefly mentioned,. Since these are the measurements used in the field in child development, it would be useful to cover these aspects in more detail.

(3) The weight for height measurement was explained in more detail, although this measurement is not used in the field at present.

Training session plan 5

Topic : Causes of Diarrhoea and its prevention.

Objectives : To involve the trainees in an analysis of the causes of diarrhoea among children, its prevention and management.

Target group : Child Development Functionaries

No. of trainees : 30

Training time : 45 minutes to 1 hour

Methods/strategies used-Analytical method

Audio-visual Aids/materials

required - (1) Two poster-

(i) Healthy Child

(ii) Child suffering from diarrhoea

(2) Tow sets of small card-

(i) showing various causes leading to dirrhoea

(ii) showing healthy practices that lead to the prevention of diarrhea.

Summary of content

(1) Preparation of material

(a) Prepare two poster on thick paper. One poster represents a child suffering from diarrhoea and the other an healthy child.

(b) On small chart are depicted different causes of diarrhoea such as dirty surroundings, unclean water, flies sitting on food, a child defecating in open, bottle feeding etc.

The other set of cards show ways to prevent Diarrhoea in children such as giving oral rehydration solution, a mother breast-feeding her baby, boiling, water, clean surroundings, washing of hands before preparing food etc.

(c) The posters are put on the wall or blackboard.

Activity

Training session Plan 6

Topic : Common feeding practices, food fads and fallacies among the vulnerable groups.

Objectives : (i) To find out the local food beliefs and practices prevalent among young children, pregnant and lactation mother.

What the trainer does	*What the trainees do*
1) The trainer shows the chart of the sick child with diarrhoea and asks the trainees to interpret the poster.	1) The trainess say that the poster shown is that of a child suffering form diarrhoea.

2) The poster of the healthy child is shown to the trainees who are asked to interpret the chart.	2) The trainees explain the visual on the chart.
3) The trainers places small cards on the table and asks the trainees to select small cards and place these next to the posters they are related to giving reasons for doing so.	3) The trainees, one by one pick up cards and place these against the appropriate poster.
4) The trainer then asks as to what measures could be taken by the trainees to prevent diarrhoea in their community.	4) The trainees enumerate the causes and preventive measures for diarrhoea.
5) The trainer guides the discussions giving additional information as and when required.	5) The trainees take down notes wherver necessary.

(ii) To create understanding about food beliefs and practices which may have harmful or beneficial effects.

Trainees : Child Development worker.

Member of trainees : 25 trainees.

Training time : 1 hours 15 minutes.

Training method used : Introductory talk followed by buzzing in small groups followed by group discussion.

Training process : In this method the group in divided

into small sub-groups which discuss a topic simultaneously after initial introduction to the subject by the trainer.

Since the fad, fallacies and feeding practices very form place to place, this method is used so that maximum examples from different places which are relevant to the group could be discussed so that the group will have a comparative view of the various feeding practices prevalent in different areas.

The group is introduced to some of the feeding practices, fads and fallacies which are given as examples. Once they understand these terms, they are divided into four sub-groups. It is ensured that each group is a mixed one with regard to age, sex, religion, state they represent, etc.

Each sub-group is asked to discuss the feeding practices, fads and fallacies for the vulnerable group prevalent in their areas, One person in each group is asked to take down unedited responses of the group members.

At the end of about 20 minutes of buzz seminar when the participants have listed down their responses, one person from each group is asked to present to the plenary, the points which they have noted down. Each practice, fad and fallacy is discussed with the group by the trainer on the following points.

i) Whether it is a positive or negative or negative practice.

ii) Whether we need to encourage or discourage the practice or leave it alone, in case it is harmless or not related to health and nutrition.

iii) How the practices can be promoted if it is

scientifically correct and the wrong beliefs which may have harmful effects removed form the community social practices.

Training session plan 7

Topic	:	Introduction of Supplementary foods in an infant diet.
Objectives	:	To understand the need and importance of giving supplementary foods to infants.
Trainees	:	Child development workers 30 trainees
Session time	:	1 hour
seating Arrange	:	Classroom
Training method	:	Open ended story and group discussion used
Training Aids used	:	Maxiflans/Puppets

Open ended stories are often used to excite the analytical thinking where in participants are encouraged to react to a conflicting situation. In the open ended story, there are two or three characters with one central character. This central character is exposed to different conflicting ideas generated by other characters in the story. The main character is thus undecided in the story. The trainer than pose questions to the group. The varied reactions of the trainees usually provoke discussions full solution of the problem to complete the story through a series of steps like observation, reasoning, classification, comparison, discussion and decision making.

In this context, the trainer uses open ended story on the topic' Introducing supplementary foods in an infants diet.'

Story characters

1) Raju : Eight month old infant
2) Kamala : Raju's mother
3) Papu : Seven month old infant
4) Vimala : Papu's mother and Kamala's friend
5) Geeta : Friend and neighbour of Kamala and Vimala
6) Dadima : Kamala'mother-in-law

A brief on open ended story on the topic with characters as mentioned above:

As the story progresses, each character when mentioned , appears from either behind the curtain as a puppet, or on the flannel as a maxiflan.

Story

"Kamala is very happy that she has been blessed with bonny son. She very lovingly breast-feeds the baby Raju. Its son is growing up into a healthy baby. But, as the months puss, she notices that Raju cries a lot and is not growing well and losing weight.

Raju is now eight months old, a thin, week child who cries a lot. Raju is a sharp contrast to her dream baby. Kamala is very sad an worried.

One day, Kamala goes to her friend Vimala, in the same village, she is very surprised and happy to see Vimala's son papu, who is a healthy, chubby and happy seven-month-old infant. Kamala asks Vimala the secret of Papu's health and narrates how her Raju, even though older to Papu by one month, is a week and unhealthy child.

Vimala reveals that since her son was four months old, she started giving him semi-solid food in the form of soft cooked cereals, pulses, vegetables and fruits in addition to her own milk which she regularly fed him. He suggests that Kamala should start giving Raju similar foods and also show him to the doctor in the Primary. Health Centre. When Kamala talks to her mother-in-law about giving semi-solid food to Raju, she is rebuked by her and told that she had brought up so may children but had not started them on solids before they were one year old.

While Kamala and Vimala are talking to each other, Geeta joins. Geeta looks at Raju and exclaims in surprise at his poor health. She tells Kamala that it seems that some one has cast an "evil eye" on Raju and that Kamala must immediately take Raju to Vasanti, a quack in the village.

Kamala wants her child to be healthy but is very confused. She does not know what to do or whose advice to follow.

Discussion

At this point, the trainer stops the narration or the story and poses Kamala"s problem to the trainees and invites their reactions. The varied responses of the trainees are noted down such as:

i) Kamala should go to the village quack

ii) She should give semi-solid foods to Raju in addition to breast milk.

iii) She should consult a doctor, etc.

iv) She should take the advice of Dadima Who is experienced in bringing up children.

The trainer then arranges these in order of scientifically appropriate responce, giving last priority to the responses ridden with superstition. the trainer thus guides the story to wards a meaningful completion supplementing it with necessary information on the subject and explaining wrong beliefs and practice.

This method is very useful and effective in getting the message across as the conclusions guided by the trainer are considered as "their own" by the trainees and hence quickly adapted by the group.

Training session plan 8

Topic : Assessment of nutritional status of children using weight and mid-arm circumference measurement criteria,

Trainer : Ms, Punam Ohri

Behavioural Objectives : To help the trainees develop skills for

1) using tricoloured mid-arm circumference measurement tape.
2) measuring the weight of children using a salter weighing scale.
3) assessing the correct age of children.
4) plotting the weight of children on growth chart and
5) interpreting the growth curve correctly and suggesting appropriate action.

Trainees : Child Development workers

Number of trainees : 30

Session time : 2 hour 30 minutes

Seating arrange : the trainees were seated in rows in the Nutrition laboratory.

Method used : Brain storming, demonstration and practicals.

Audio visual aids and

Materials used : 1) Tricoloured mid-arm circumference tape

2) Salter weighing scale

3) Local events calender

4) Enlarged growth chart on flannel

5) Work book on weight plotting

Training process : The trainer proceeded with the session as follows:

what trainer does	*What the trainees do*
1) The trainer gave a brief introduction on measurement of growth and asked the trainees the need for the mesurementh of growth. What the trainees do	The trainees gave various answers regarding why the growth should be measured.
2) The trainer summarises the answers given by the trainees on the board.	The trainess take down notes.
3) The trainer explains the correct use of tricoloured tape and weight for age criteria in assessing the nutritional statues.	The trainees take down notes.
4) The trainer brain-stormed the trainees to find out which of the two methods explained above was better for the assessment of nutritional status and why.	Most of the trainees give the correct answer.
5) The trainer summarises the advantages and disadvantages of the two methods.	The trainees observe keenly. the also study the salter scale which is passed on the them.

6) The trainer demonstrates the method of weighing children using a salter weighing scale and taking the reading.	The trainees give various answers.
7) The trainer asks the trainees about various methods that they could use for assessing the age of a child.	The trainees look at the local events calender being circulated and take notes.
8) The trainer jots down all the answers and explains their use. the trainer then explained the use of local evens calendar.	The trainees take down notes and observe.
9) The trainer explains the Plotting of weights on the flannel growth chart using the weight and age examples.	The rest of the trainess observe.
10) The trainer invites one of the trainees to plot a given weight on the growth chart.	The trainees observe
11)The trainer demonstrates the use of mind-arm circumference tape..	The trainees take down notes and answer the questions asked by the trainer.
12)The trainer explains the interpretation of the growth curve as also of the coloured band, and asks that questions to ensure the trainees have grasped it.	The trainees take down notes.
13)The trainer re-emphasises the correction of zero-error before weighing on salter scale as also the correct position at which the mid- arm circumference tape to be used.	The trainees start doing the exercises.

14) The trainees start doing the workbooks on weight plotting to the trainees and asks them to do the exercise, 15) Trainer asks the trainees to simultaneously assess the nutritional status of some children using the tricoloured tape and confirm the assessment by weighing the children on a salter scale. The trainer also tells them as to how to standardize the weighing scale at frequent intervals.	The trainees use the tricoloured tape and salter weighing scale for the assessment of nutritional status of children. This way done in batches of four while others completed the exercises in the workbook. Each trainee weighed at least one child and measured the mid arm cercumference of at least one child. The rest of the trainees in each batch observed and pointed out the mistakes committed by the one actually weighing an measuring the mid-arm circumference.

Comments and suggestions

1) The method and aids used for this session are suitable, as the trainees see to comprehend what is being explained.
2) The flannel growth chart should be on the board.
3) Coloured thread, board pins, or coloured dots could be used to show a couple of weight plottings on the flannel growth chart.
4) Some aids like wooden rods, models of arm made with stuffed cotton, rolled, chart, stufied toys, papers et of varying drametre could be used for practicing the use of mid-arm circumference tape and its interpretation.

Training Session Plan

Topic : Use of waste material for making/learning/teaching aids for preschool work

Behavioural objectives

Trainees will be able to:

i) identify waste from the surroundings.

ii) make use of waste in preparation of inexpensive teaching aids for organising preschool activities.

Target group

The group is already engaged in training child care workers in preschool education. Hetrerogeneous in age and educational background the lowest educational qualification is graduation.

Number of trainees	: 33
Training time	: 3 hours
Audio visual Aids/ materials	: no Audio-visual aids used

Observations and comments

(1) Guided practical session is an appropriate method considering objectives of the session.

(2) It is a deviation form a normal talk and chalk method or other practical sessions where raw material is provided to the trainees. The fact that the trainees are asked to collect the waste within the time allotted for the session ensured the trainees involvement from the very beginning.

(3) The limitations of this methods lie in the fact that it is only one time session. Though each trainee is given a chance to talk and explain their presentation, There is no time for the discussion by the trainees not is there time for summarising the entire session by the trainer.

Since the waste material is collected on the spot, there is not much variety, therefore the charts made are more or less of the same type. Besides the learning points highlighted by these charts do not cover all the points. The participants do not get enough time to learn the use of waste material in different aspects of development. Thus though the methodology followed is appropriate the allocation of time is not sufficient to achieve the behavioural objectives.

Suggestion
More time is to be allocated for this learning unit. Discussion and summarising learning points may consolidate learning gains. Use of the material made by the trainees will help them learn from each other's comments/suggestions/difficulties.

Training session plan 10

Topic : Common nutritional deficiency diseases and their management.

Behavioural : (1) To familiarise the trainess with various nutritional deficiency diseases-PEM, Vitamin A, Anaemia etc.

(2) To enable them to identify symptoms of the common deficiency diseases.

(3) To familiarise the trainees with the prevention and management of these deficiency diseases.

Target Group: Child Development Workers,

Number of trainees : 30

Training time: 1 hour 15 minutes

Seating arrangement. : The trainees are seated in semi-circular rows in a classroom.

Audio-visual Aids and Materials: Project of black and white as also coloured slides showing symptoms of various nutritional deficiencies.

Training process : Lecture supplemented by pictures and chalk and talk.

What the trainer does	*What the trainees do*
(1) The trainer lists out various nutrients and the related deficiency diseases on the blackboard using simple words.	The trainees take down notes.
(2) The trainer explains the terms as also shows the picture of each deficiency disease.	The trainees take down the notes.
(3) Each deficiency disease is dealt separately by the trainer giving causes, signs and symptoms by listing on board and projecting visuals through the epidiascope.	The trainees take down notes and occasionally ask the trainer to eaplain the technical terms, if any, in the presentation.
(4) The terms are explained by the trainer	Trainees take down the notes.
(5) The trainer indicate the weight of the child on the growth chart to show the stage where the child gets malnourished.	Trainees take down the notes.
(6) The trainer notes on the board, a checklist of signs and symptoms of malnutrition.	The trainees take down the notes.

(7) The trainer asks the food sources of various nutrients.	The trainees tell the food sources.
(8) The trainer then explains what foods should be given in increased amounts to prevent and manage the nutritional deficiency diseases.	The trainees take down the notes.

Suggestions

(1) In the management of deficiency diseases, the emphasis should be made on dietary aspects of nutrition supplementation as well as on the dosage of vitamins and minerals.

(2) Some lead questions should also be asked to elicit responses from the trainees as also to ascertain whether they are understanding the topic under discussion.

Training session Plan 11

Topic : Assessment of nutritional status of children.

Objectives : To help the trainees develop skills in

(1) Using tricoloured mid-arm circumference tape for screening malnourished children.

(2) Measuring the weight of a child on salter weighing scale.

(3) Plotting the weight of a child on the growth chart, and

(4) Interpreting the growth curve correctly and suggesting appropriate action.

Trainees : Child Development Project Officers

Number of trainees: 30

Session time : 2 hours 30 minutes

Seating arrangement : The trainees were seated in the Nutrition Laboratory

Method used : Demonstration and practical work

Audio-visual aids
and materials used : (1)Enlarged growth chart on fiannel
(2) Salter weighing scale
(3) Growth charts
(4) Tricoloured mid-arm circumference tape.

Training process

The trainer gives a brief introduction about the importance of measuring and monitoring the growth of young children. She explains the different methods by which growth can be measured. She describes in detail about the use of mid-arm Circumference and weight for age methods which are simple and effective for measuring growth of young children at the field level.

The trainer puts up the enlarged fiannel growth chart and uses it as a training tool to explain to the trainees the growth chart and its correct use. She then hangs the salter scale, explains and demonstrates how to weigh children correctly on this scale and plot the weight on the growth chart. Each trainee is made to weigh two children, below 6 years and plot their weights on the growth chart after ascertaining their age. The trainees categories the children as normal, mildly, moderately or severely malnourished and note action to be taken by them in each case. The results of their weighing and interpretation are presented to the class and discussed.

The trainer gives exercises to the trainees for practicing filling up the growth chart and interpretating the growth curve. The trainer also distributes some charts which have been filled up having errors and asks the trainees to examine these and give their comments.

Practicals on measuring the upper mid-arm circumference of children in the age group of 1-5 years to screen malnourished children in the trainees is also carried out.

Training session plan 12

Topic : Mother's awareness and participation in pre-school education.

Behavioural objectives

(i) Emphasise the need and importance of involving mothers and ultimately parents and community in the pre-school work.

(ii) Learn methods of creating awareness about pre-school work.

`(iii) Learn methods of involvement of mothers parents and ultimately the community.

Number of trainees : 30-40

Training time : 1 hour 15 minutes

Seating arrangement : The trainees are to be seated in rows.

Method : Lecture-cum- discussion supported by aids.

Audio-visual aids/ material used : Black board, chalk, projector and slides.

Training process

Time	*Trainer*	*Trainee*
20 minutes	The trainer introduces the topic, explains its importance and its contours for five minutes.	The trainer ask question which are answered by the trainer.
	The trainer asks a question about the rationale of the need for mothers involvement in the preschool education work.	The trainees listen and then respond.
	The trainer lists the The trainees take down points in favour of mother's awareness about pre-school education as under: i) The survival, growth and development of the child is basically the responsibility of the mother. ii) Mother is nearest to the child. iii) Pre-school centre is the extension of the home.	

iv) The pre-school child spends 20 out of 24 hours in the home particularly with the mother and only 4 hours in the pre-school centre.

The traines take down these points written by the trainer on the black board.

The Trainer explains that:

i) It is not necessary for the mothers to be educated to be aware of the need and importance of pre-school education.

The trainees ask him to educate the illiterate mothers.

ii) It is also not necessary all the time for the mothers to come to the centre if they are not free. Other sibling-grand-mother, elder sister, etc. representing.

The family could come on their behalf, failing which any other mother may exchange the turn with the mother who is unable to come on a particular day.

The trainer lists on the board the following method:

i) The mock nursery class should be held with the mothers.

ii) The mothers should be made familiar with the equipment and material used in the pre-school centre.

iii) Mothers should be made to prepare the material to be used in the pre-school situations.

The trainees were then convinced that it was possible and desirable to involve the mothers, parents and the community in the work of pre-school centre

10

Management and Approaches to Training

Judging from the large number of management and supervisory training programs published and promoted during the 1960s, this area of training became the primary center of attention for organizations selling training services. In the 1970s this growth has continued with further increases in management models and approaches as well as a growing interest in career planning and development. During the 1950s, the greatest apparent growth took place in sales training efforts, but today the consultant have turned to improving the performance of people who "get things done through others". Whether these programs have dealt with "first-line supervisor" or with "managers of managers," interest in them points out the conscious expression of a need on the part of organizations employing them.

The term "supervisory training" implies that some kind of behavior change is the objective factions taken and that further, the performance change resulting from those actions will be planned and evaluated in terms of some sort of performance standards. Such training may be used as part of a management-development system, but not as a substitute for actions directed at individual long-term growth. Whereas management-development actions are designed and implemented to concentrate on the strengths of individuals who already meet or exceed some sort of a standard, training actions are directed at substandard or nonexistent performance in a significant group of supervisory employees. In the first instance, management says, "Find our best people-those with the greatest potential-and get them ready for new or additional responsibilities""; in the second instance, management is saying, "We are not getting the kind of performance we expect or need from a particular group of employees. Find a way to bring them up to our standards.

Difficulty of supervisory training

From the beginning, supervisory training programs have little chance for success in terms of behavior change. There are formidable problems when we try to define the supervisor's job in terms of performance. Determining what a first-line supervisor or a middle manager does is not a matter of textbook definition; the job varies from organization to organization and within the organization from system to system. Even within a system it will vary from one time to another. To say that a supervisor is one who gets work done through others is an oversimplification and not altogether usable. This tells us not what a supervisor does, but rather that what he or she "does" will be measured through the performance of those supervised. Yet this is not usually a fact. If it were, a supervisor's performance would be measured by the individual outputs of the people reporting to him or her. But supervisors are not usually measured by the individual outputs of their subordinates. At best, this performance is measured in terms of the total outputs of the group supervised and at worst, by ability to avoid "exceptions" which require the intervention of superiors.

It is conceivable that a supervisor of a group of inventory clerks, for example, could obtain all of the results required of the clerical group by doing the work personally. If the group's objectives were set low enough, a few extra hours of work on the part of the supervisor would make any activities on the part of the clerks unnecessary. Certainly in this case the work would not be done through others. There would be no delegation of work would not be done through others. There is an extremely poor supervisor, yet the requirements of the system are met! Impossible as this appears, it is at least partially true in the cases of many supervisors and managers who do not delegate a significant portion of decision making or work production to their people. In fact, it is considered a common ailment of those promoted through levels of management that they carry upward certain operational work better delegated to people reporting to them.

In one organization, first-line supervisors may have no supervisory duties at all. They may instead be troubleshooters for breakdowns, supertechnicians who advise setup people on the proper installation and adjustment of jigs and dies, or perhaps messengers between the general supervisor and the machine operator to deliver task assignments and other instructions. In some organizations the supervisor's job is so proceduralized that there are no options in behavior allowed. In fact, in the event that a situation arises for which there is no procedure, the general supervisor or superintendent is apprised and makes decisions. On the other hand, some organizations expect quite a bit from a supervisor, giving that person the freedom to make a large number of decisions at his or her own discretion and to carry out necessary actions, reporting to superiors only when particular problems occur. In some instances even greater authority is delegated, and the supervisor makes regular reports to management on the status of assignments.

The job of a middle manager is as varied as that of a supervisor. The traditional view that the job of a manager is to plan, organize, direct, coordinate, and control the work of others permits a unified approach to training, but does not provide an objective definition of managerial tasks. Lacks of objectification of the tasks and roles of supervisors and the failure to provide measurable performance standards make it difficult to structure training. If a means could be found to work toward rational and applicable behavior criteria for supervisors, there would be a wide range of potential missions for training. First, supervisory training could be the means for bringing about technical and organizational change in the management of an organization; that is, training could be the agency to bring about system modifications such as the introduction of computer technology or automation. Second, it could also be the means for bringing about changes in the management structure itself, perhaps permitting delegation of greater decision-making authority at lower levels, potentially eliminating layers of middle management. Third, it could be the agency for selecting and preparing individuals for promotion to supervision. Thus training could become a powerful tool for the acquisition and maintenance of supervisory personnel. Fourth, it could serve as a change agency to bring the individual behavior of supervisory personnel up to the established standards of performance. Fifth, it could be an agency for coordinating the efforts of a number of supervisors, taking the form of "team training" to develop a higher degree of cooperative spirit within an organization and greater goal centering of various interfacing sub systems. Finally, it could serve as an agency for attitude change, to bring about the desirable condition of have even the lowest levels of supervision, traditionally caught between the work force and upper levels of management by their role demands, adopt and attitude which would place them fully within the "management camp". This last mission has the potential for developing more satisfying human relations between peers and with subordinates.

Training middle managers

The middle manager presents a most difficult problem in the determination of training needs. This results from the wide discrepancies between system requirements and management expectations and between each of these and the expectations of the supervisors themselves. Throughout this book the basic premise has been that when performance is unacceptable, it is due to behavior different from that which is necessary to obtain the results the system requires. For most training actions, the system requirements alone can determine behavioral-change needs. The organization's management sees individual performance as directly related to a set of observable results in terms of system requirements. Behavior is proximate to the results. Thus the salespersons's performance produces orders' the secretary's, letters? the press operator's, processed stock. In all of these situations, performance can be defined in terms of system requirements. As for manager or supervisor performance, we can say that the system requirements are imposed, because in order to produce the expected results, any operating system must have certain functions performed and certain actions taken, and some of these functions or actions are assigned to individuals in supervisory capacities.

But the behavior of individuals assigned to management or supervisory functions often affects the system design itself, due to the wide variance between system requirements and management's view of the supervisor's roles. From the chief executive down the supervisor's superiors all expect certain kinds of performance. Management may expect the same supervisor to make operator assignments in a "fair" manner, so as to avoid grievances or work slowups. To the supervisor, the job is one of "keeping everyone busy". Here is the dilemma : In order to meet system requirements, the supervisor must be "unfair," because of the need to show favoritism to the most skilled, most efficient, and most motivated workers, placing them in key tasks. Every attempt to meet the needs of the system can result in charges of favoritism, and as far as management expectations are concerned, performance will be susbstandard; that is, the supervisor will be demonstrating poor "human relations." Most often, system requirements are ignored by the supervisor and the over-all performance of the production system is affected. It should not be surprising that where there is a difference, the supervisor is more likely to meet management's expectations than the system's requirements. After all, in most production systems there is maximum feedback from the supervisor's superiors, usually quite direct and quite immediate, whereas seldom is the supervisor wholly part of the feedback loop of the system design itself.

The discrepancies are further increased because of the management group's emotional involvement in defining supervisory performance. Upper-level managers look at those below as though they themselves were still in these positions, and all too frequently they define these roles and performances in terms of their idealization of them. One organization uses the supervisor as a firing-line decision maker, participating in shaping the destinies of the organisation; another see the supervisor as a necessary evil who rides herd on a lazy and incompetent work force.

Defining supervisory training needs

The trainer is faced with the monumental task of translating these often irrational idealizations of

SUPERVISORY performance into training criteria which can be met and accepted as measure of performance. The key to developing training actions for supervisory performance is the analysis process. Analysis will bring together system requirements and the various expectations to a point where performance can be identified. It will also develop standards acceptable to management, and ideally it will meet system requirements. At the very least, analysis will bring to the attention of management discrepancies between system requirements and management expectations. If there is no possibility of bringing them together or changing one to conform to the other, the trainer, in consultation with management, will be able to defend the supervisor from performance measures which require unobtainable to defend the supervisor from performance measures which require unobtainable behaviour. The analysis, then, will provide a set of required behaviors together with their related actual behaviors. It will result in a set of requirements to be met by changes in the system, in performance expectations, or in individual behaviors. Any changes brought about should be acceptable to management and at the same time contribute to meeting organizational goals, missions, and objectives.

Following such an analysis from beginning to end is probably the best way to examine the kinds of problems which will be encountered. We might first consider a project involving fist-line supervision in a manufacturing system. In this case the project under discussion was requested by the organization's chief executive and an operating committee consisting of key staff and the general managers of the manufacturing divisions involved. This first step, gaining an operational commitment from general management, may be thought of as the first gating factor for any project involving supervision. Therefore, before any further action can be planned, the objective of the project will have to be established, and the trainer will have to receive not only the approval, but also the acceptance, of top management.

The objectives of this project were to provide the company with an analysis of the foreman's job in the "A" manufacturing division so that the company could: (1) specify the job of the foreman; (2) relate the job of foreman functionally to the goals of the division; (3) redesign the position of foreman to make it a more effective component of the division in terms of system requirements; (4) set performance standards and measures for a foreman; (5) establish criteria for foreman selection; and (6) conduct training relevant to the foreman's job as it exists or as it might be redesigned. In endorsing objectives like these, general management accepts the possible consequences of the analysis, namely, that change actions may be expressed not only as training needs but also as changes in the expectations of the systems or of management. Management will anticipate recommendations for job redesign or redefinition and, ideally, by endorsing these objectives will be open to such recommendations.

Considering real-world problems, the implications of these objectives could be a considerable threat for the management of the system which will be investigated. It is relatively easy for a member of management to accept a first-or second-line supervisor's performance as resulting from lack of ability or poor attitude. But it is often difficult to accept the possibility that substandard performance is due to the organization's structure which he or she has personally designed or to conflicts created by permitting wide discrepancies between system requirements and personal expectations of the supervisor's performance. Yet if effective training is to take place in this kind of situation, the trainer must avoid being trapped into limiting analysis to the upper levels of management; in other words the trainer must not take the easy route of looking to the plant manager for descriptions of what supervisors do on the job, but actually work with the supervisors. At the same time, the trainer will have to work very closely with members of management in the system to gain their commitment as the analysis proceeds. The trainer must not be guilty of cutting management people out of the feedback loop.

Analysis of supervisory training needs

In the project under discussion, the first step in maintaining a close interface/ communications/feedback relationship with the managers involved meant developing a well-defined project design which detailed a series of required feedbacks to management. The system model for the project looked like that . The model follows the entire project from the first step of scheduling through the completion of all proposed training actions. It breaks down into three main subsystems: the analysis itself, the development of a foreman selection action, and the development and implementation of foreman training actions.

With this overall project model, management was given a task schedule carefully outlining the approval points. These approval points are decision junctions at which the system's management was called on to approve the project's outputs.

There are two reasons for presenting this kind of schedule to both the general manager and the subject division manager. First, it lets them know what to expect and assures them that they will participate in every important decision. Second, it gives them a means for measuring the training function's performance, for they can use this schedule as a statement of target dates for each of the outputs expected during the course of the project.

Elements one through five of mode comprise the analysis portion of the project system. The output for element one is, of course, the schedule itself, which will describe the kinds of outputs management may expect and give the target dates for them. Element two, the system analysis, results in a report to management identifying change needs of the division under investigation. When this analysis is completed and the needs both specified and summarized, the report is presented to the company's chief executive and the manager of the subject division for their confirmation and approval. The confirmation comes from a mutual discussion of the report's contents and an attempt to obtain management's agreement that the report validly describes the manufacturing system. Agreement means that management accepts these facts and understands the relationship to the performance of the foremen. The agreement precedes the next element of the training system-completion of a selection and training proposal. The output of this element is a general strategy acceptable to management for bringing about the changes required by the system.

Table : Feedback and approval schedule: Forman project

Task	Traget [Plus ( ) Calendar Days]
1. Project schedule approved by president and division general manager	(7)
2. Report of change needs and recommendations presented to president and division general manager	(36)

3. Selection and training proposal approved by division general manager (36)
4. Performance standards approved by division general manager (48)
5. Selection criteria approved by division general manager (63)
6. Foreman assessments reported to division general manager (77)
7. Training objectives approved by division general manager and reviewed by president (84)
8. Training plan approved by division general manager (90)
9. Selection-team training-program evaluation reported to division general manager (156)
10. Foreman training-program evaluation reported to division general manager (300)
11. Foreman candidates list approved by division general manager (224)

The proposal is important for a number of reasons. The general procedure to be followed must be approved and accepted by management, since further investment in time and money will be required. The proposal itself is the basis for all future planning for the balance of the project and determines the kinds of change actions selected. This kind of proposal makes it necessary for the two levels of management involved to not only participate in the selection of strategies, but also make a commitment to the proposed investment.

The fourth element requires the development of performance standards and criteria, the basis for evaluation of the training actions and for evaluation and assessment of the supervisors in training and on the job.

A set of performance standards, together with measurements, is presented to management for its approval.

The fifth element of the analysis portion produces criteria for selecting new foremen, and again the approval of both levels of management is required (element six), since considerable commitment will be made toward the shaping of future supervision in the organization.

As a result of the processes carried out in the seventh element of the system, a selection team is brought together and trained to use the planned presupervisory training program as a foreman-selection medium. The actual selection of team members is made by the division manager, drawing individuals from among the general foremen, production superintendents, and members of the division staff. Thus the direct participation of the division manager in carrying out the processes of this element is quite explicit. It become important, therefore, to plan the division manager's attendance in a test run of the presupervisory training and selection team itself can provide the necessary feedbacks to the division manager on progress in the candidate-evaluation reports. In effect, the staff trainers involved in the project will be turning over actual operation of the selection program and the presupervisory training program to the division manager for delegation, in this case to the selection team.

The tenth element produces a performance assessment of each foreman within the division. This assessment is an evaluation of performance against the performance standards in element four and the selection criteria developed in element important in obtaining further commitment, so that there will be confidence in the ability of this process to validly make performance assessments. Obviously, each assessment report will go to the division manager, and the plan includes a detailed discussion of as many of these assessments as necessary. A summary report on over-all performance of foremen in the division is made jointly by the staff trainer and the division manager to the company's chief executive to ensure key feedback on overall performance at the top.

Element eleven will produce a detailed set of training objectives and criteria statements to be given to both the chief executive and the division manager of the subject division. Their approval is necessary at this point, and these statements will provide the staff trainers with an opportunity to describe the limitations of the behaviors to be produced in the formal training action and permit them to recommend a reinforcement system to be carried out on the job. With the recommendations accepted, instructional design can being; the next feedback should be a dry run of the training actions, with the division manager and possibly the company chief executive participating as means to gain their future commitment to the processes.

From this point forwards, the evaluation reports implied in element fifteen will be communicated to the chief executive and the division manager and discussed in detail with them to give them confidence that the planned changes are coming about. These planned feedbacks to the decision-making levels of management are intended to force participation in the training action by line management. This involvement is more critical in supervisory training action by line management. This involvement is more critical in supervisory training than in any other training effort. There must be commitment to not only the specific actions to be taken, but also the philosophy or style of the underlying management approaches. The system model points out that if all of these processes are going to take place, new performance standards, behavioral criteria, and assessment processes will have to be developed, which will have far-reaching implications for supervisory performance in the organization. The training actions, then, cannot be separated from the normal operation of this particular division. The project plan has as part of its intention the integration of selection and training with other management processes.

Setting up a task model

The task model used for carrying out the analysis of change needs for this project consists of ten task elements. The model could be used as a general approach to analysis for any subject of training, with the possible exception of the tasks involving organisation relationships. The latter are less appropriate to industrial skill and administrative skill raining, which do not normally impose such demands These tasks become important in undertaking analysis for supervisory training, because the supervisor is involved in far more formal and informal organizational relationships which have far more effect on performance than do the limited interfaces of an individual machine operator or administrative employee.

The first task is the development of a formal organizational model with the objective of determining management's view of the foremen who are the subject showing the reporting authority and accountability relationships one level below and one level above the foreman in the organizational line and those functional relationships which management recognizes as including the subject foremen. If a formal organizational chart exists, its contents must be confirmed through interviews with the division manager and staff members who have the authority to recommend changes or make revisions in the formal relationships. If an organizational chart does not exist, the training analyst must work with these same sources to create one.

The second task develops an "operating" organizational model to determine the relationships really required to get the job done. This results in an organizational chart showing the actual interfaces, feedback point, and control points with which the foreman is involved. Thus this task identifies the differences between management's formal view of the organization and the actual operating organization. The task would include interviews with managers of functional units designated in the formal organizational chart, members of their departments, and interviews with foremen and general foremen to identify the organizational relationships they see and use.

In creating this model, the analyst will attempt to describe not only the recognized organizational relationships, but also relationships imposed by the various informal demands of the organization. In the example used here, one such description highlights the fact that the informal organizational relationships built up over a period of time forced a significant number of assembly department foremen into the position of having no direct authority over lift-truck operators, thought by higher levels of management to be reporting directly to these foremen-at least, that is what the organizational chart showed! Actually, however, an informal coordinating function had grown up in production control as a cost-reduction effort to decrease the number of truck operators. This had taken place a some previous time when production demands were lower, but there were no changes as the assembly demands had increased. The foremen were now faced with using their powers of persuasion to compete with fellow foremen for the services of the operators. Since some of the foremen involved were relatively new to the organization, they thought that this was part of the formal structure - "the way we do things here".

The third task develops the flow of materials through the system in order to identify the points at which supervisory action is required to move or process material. The output of this task is a flow model showing the movement of material from the point of receipt through shipping, from beginning to end. This task is carried out on the floor following the processes in their physical reality. Then it is checked against the model of production flow of the processing engineering department or industrial engineering department, which in the example was available to the analyst. Interviews are carried out with production scheduling and production control functions and with individual foremen, with question such as: "Where do you get your processed stock? Where do you start? How do you know you're going to get it at the right time and in the right quantities? If it's not where it's supposed to be, where do you go to find it?" etc.

The fourth task develops an information flow model similar to the material flow model, but has the objective of identifying the supervisor's information points. Incorporating information formats and sources, the output is a flow chart showing the major information models of information about material, people, controls, and facilities. The task is carried out through a series of interviews with members of the functions involved and with the line supervisors, using questions such as " If you are supposed to set priorities for the operation of your department, how do you know how to set those priorities? What schedules do you us? What other information do you receive? May I see copies of the?" etc. The analyst follows each formal communications medium, tracking each copy of it and making notes about changes in content, ending up with flow models of such things as production cards, time cards, production schedules, schedule explosions, scrap reports, maintenance job histories, downtime reports, and the like.

Task five is to make a functional analysis of the supervisory jobs. Using the data developed in the first four tasks, the analyst determines management expectations and system requirements for each function involved. The outputs are descriptions of all systems relating to first line supervisors that describe the missions, outputs, input requirements, sources for those inputs, interface points, feedback points, feedback media, and methods presently used to measure the performance of the function or methods which might be proposed for such measurements. These outputs become a basic tool in developing recommendations for changes not involving training. Improvement in feedback, for example, so that foremen will have more timely and accurate information about their performance, is probably the most frequent kind of system change recommendation that will be made, and it grows from the data developed in this task.

The sixth task is to make supervisory performance analyses in order to determine current performance and current performance standards. A further objective is the identification of performance items in the behavioral terms "can do" and "will do". For example, part of the task will be to identify substandard or nonexistent performance which is either expected or required in the present system and to find out whether individuals involved have the necessary skills or knowledge to carry out the tasks required, or whether their substandard performance is due to other causes such as improper or invalid information, unacceptable attitude, or conflicting demands. The outputs of this task are descriptions of existing supervisory performance in terms of responsibilities, accountabilities, authorities, decision points, feedback point, performance standards, and performance measures. The task is carried out through a series of interviews, with selected foremen talking to their superiors about their subordinates, to their subordinates about their superiors, to subordinates about other subordinates, and to the subordinates about them selves. If enough supervisors are subject to the training project, then a random selection could probably be made to cover about 20% of the foreman group. If the total number of foremen involved is too small to allow confidence in random selection, a useful tactic could be to talk to the most experienced and least experienced, two of the best and two of the worst, youngest and oldest, making sure every function is covered so that variances in job requirements can be identified and considered in making the analysis.

Task seven develops performance standards to be used in identifying performance areas that require some kind of change action. The analyst's objective here is to establish workable performance standards. The standards developed in the analysis task will be validated in terms of the organization as it is. A set of measurable performance standards forms the output of this task: Outputs from tasks five and six are compared, giving a picture of actual performance as it relates to total system requirements and management expectations. The analyst will be attempting to identify critical performance standards and to develop some reasonable means to measure the performance. A very close working relationship is needed here between the training analyst and the division manager and probably each level of supervision down to the foreman. These standards will, after all, form the most critical basis for decisions about foreman performance, and the organization's management must be committed to them if any training actions are to be successful.

From these standards, the analyst will go on to task eight and develop performance criteria. Here the output will be a set of criteria to be used in evaluating performance in the organization as it exists. These criteria will be used to measure existing performance in terms of the standards developed in task seven.

Task nine validates these criteria in order to establish management's confidence that the criteria do adequately and validly measure performance in the organization. Again, a sampling of incumbent foremen is used, on either a random basis or by selection of a worst-to-best performers range. Identification of best and worst can be made subjectively by general supervision and/or production management personnel. In essence, the analyst is asking, "Who is your best person? Who is your worst? Who is your next best? Your next worst?" Subjective evaluation or ranking is, after all, the means the organization presently uses to measure performance. The analyst is attempting to validate the objective criteria develop by means of the subjective measures in use in the organization. If, after performance evaluation, there is a wide discrepancy between objective criteria and the subjective value judgements of the managers, it will be necessary for the analyst to go more deeply into system requirements and to test performance against those requirements. If the criteria prove valid in terms of real system requirements, the analyst then has the opportunity to persuade members of management to adopt the objective criteria as more accurate, and therefore more useful, management tools.

When the analyst finally has workable criteria which are accepted by management, the task of identifying training problems can begin. The objective is the identification of those areas of behavior that cause the substandard performance. The complexity of dealing with supervisory training problems then becomes very clear as performance problems are finally identified. The analyst finds, for example, that the system requires production foremen to maintain a specified production level as material is processed through their departments. In the course of this analysis, the analyst discovers that a significant number of the foremen are failing to meet this requirement : Their performances are substandard. After following the material and information flows through their departments, the analyst finds that indeed, the foremen's performances are substandard, but the degree below standard is unknown because there is no accurate standard for production levels. (Consider, for example, the job-shop operation making a wide variety of related products.) The foreman involved do not know what their standards are; they have no information regarding performance in terms of production requirements. In fact, from their point of view, the major portion of their job is devoted to the prevention of machine shutdowns through breakdown or setups. Foremen face a wide range of problems: They must relay on other departments to supply them with parts; they must rely on their own judgments is matter of scrapping and reworking processed goods; they must face a final line inspection which has the authority to close down their lines; they must obtain setup services which they may not control; they even have to spend a great deal of time trying to find the lift-ruck operator who can bring the stock to their areas. In this kind of situation, what, indeed, are the training needs? The analyst may propose a number of system changes to provide the foremen with feedback which can give them the kind of information they need to identify the problems in their own performance and in their departments further system changes might be recommended to give the foremen more control over the people and materials they need to get their job done. If some of these system changes can be effected, the analyst will be able to identify some very specific training needs: The may need to be brought to a skill level at which they can identify substandard work in process, so their decisions on scrap and rework will be valid. But in this particular case, it is a foreman's lack of information that is the primary cause of substandard performance, and the analyst can make a predictable improvement if feedback can be provided.

In another situation, the analyst discovers that machine operator's performance varies, depending on departmental assignment. In other words, there is a difference in productivity level from department to department. The analyst seeks out differences in the performances of the foremen in these departments and discovers that when operator performances are below expected standard, the foremen involved seldom interact directly with their people. By itself, this is not necessarily a behavioral problem, but if the analyst discovers that there is a relationship between productivity and supervisory interaction, a "human relations" problem is likely. Yet what is that specific problem? In the course of analysis, the trainer finds that a particular foreman involved feels unable to personally influence the behavior of operators. This foreman has discovered through experience that attempts to use disciplinary procedures against them result in his "eating the warning slip". Further, although the foreman considers the operators incompetent, the analyst discovers that this foreman has never taken an action to train the operator or communicated work standards to them. The foreman never felt that this was necessary, since most of them are on incentive, anyway!

Examining alternatives for behavior change

It is at this point, perhaps, that supervisory training

presents the kind of problem that makes it so unique. There are two ranges of alternatives available: the analyst can recommend a change of procedure which would eliminate the expectation from the foreman's job or else can take action to train the foreman to "motivate" employees. The direction taken must depend entirely on the underlying management philosophy or style of the organization. Oversimplifying, the choice is between "Theory X" and "Theory Y," or possibly some shade of definition in between. Now management's commitment to the entire project becomes critical. The analyst has to exact from the chief executive of the organization a decision, possibly tentative, on the direction to be taken. Thus the approach to the supervisor's performance is profoundly affected by the organisation's concepts of what that performance should be.

If the choice is to eliminate this function from the foreman's requirements, then, of course, training is not the answer. The answer must be sought in a system redesign that will somehow remove the need for personal interaction between operators and foremen. Although this approach might not be called "soul-satisfying" to the social scientist, it has been used and found to be quite acceptable and successful. The training analyst and his or her colleagues responsible for instructional design and development can certainly assist line management in preparing a set of procedures for the interaction functions. They might, for example, use the industrial relations function to "counsel" with employees, either directly or through the bargaining unit. Or, they could use the foreman as a liaison between the operators and a special staff function responsible for maintaining "fair practices".

If, however, management decides that the foreman is to have the function of using personal influences to improve or maintain performance, the analyst will begin working on the identification criteria for use in developing training towards this end.

Entry behaviors

A further problem, often more critical in supervisory training than in any other area, involves entry behaviors - the problem of the controller promoted because she was an excellent accountant or the foreman promoted because he was every good, hardworking setup man. An accurate description of the functions performed by a supervisor is needed if a valid definition of minimum entry behaviors is to be reached. In the foreman-training project used here as an example, pressroom foremen had been selected primarily on the basis of their ability to set up dies and adjust jigs. The functional description showed that technically the press room foreman needed only to be able to identify a correct setup and to describe corrective action to an employees designated as setup person. In fact, 75% of the grievances filed in the departments involved resulted from the foreman's actually doing work on setups in violation of the union contract. The technical skill so important inselection thus contributed to substandard performance, and the application of the skill affected the system. The foreman performed setups because the setup people lacked the skills to satisfy the foreman's expectations, and foremen carrying out the tasks prevented the setup people from developing the required skills. The result was closed circle.

The analyst can recommend three alternatives : (1) that a skill requiring identification and evaluation of setup-person performance be used to "extinguish" setup skills; (2) that the foreman be punished for making a setup; or (3) that responsibility .for setup be eliminated from the foreman's function. Some from of the first recommendation would have to be considered the most likely choice. Punishing a foremen for doing what he knows he can do better than anyone else leads to a number of potentially dangerous situations. He would probably suffer the effects of incompetence and malingering on the part of the hourly people, and management would no longer be on his side. Management expects the foreman to meet performance standards, but slaps him down when he takes action to meet them. The third alternative, of course, means that the foreman would no longer control one of his basic resources; he would have to negotiate with another department for needed services. Adequate staffing and procedures would be needed and would probably add to the overhead cost of the operation.

The strategy recommended is to first assign accountability for the training of setup men to the foreman and make setup operator performance part of the measure of foreman performance. In other words, substandard performance by setup men would affect the organization's evaluation of foreman performance. Next, the foreman should be trained as a setup training expert with stress on the identification of performance, problems and the use of a training process to correct them. Finally, the foreman's superior, in this case the fabrication department superintendent, should make periodic audits of setup activities and take direct actions to recognize satisfactory performance as trainers on the part of foremen. The superintendent in this case would undergo further training in coaching and counseling activities as an effective "rewarder" through direct influence.

Change and the roles of the supervisor

This small part of the entire analysis shows the implications of any supervisory training actions; like the ripples from a stone thrown into a calm pool, they grow and grow! The complexity of system change, expectation change, and behavior change, because of their mutual dependency, must be carefully thought out and painstakingly structured. In the setup situation described above, the end result is a training program foremen can use to train setup people, a change in foreman function and responsibility, a training action for the foremen's superiors, and a change in management's view for the foreman and the foreman's roles in the organization.

What has been applied here in the case of a foreman-training project becomes even more complex when we move into the middle levels of management. The interactive elements of the jobs involved are more complex, and the role demands on those in management positions are increasingly complex and less clearly defined. The role that analysis plays in defining and revising the existing organization systems can be seen as a potentially powerful management tool. The involvement of top management in the analysis process must be secured and their commitment made part of the trainer's course of action.

Any approach to training in the field of social development is a function of the philosophy that provides its under-pinnings. As social development involves ever-expanding knowledge of social processes, attitudinal transformation and skill sophistication, the training programme necessarily calls for designing and structuring to assign due place to these considerations. However, differing emphasis is provided to these components as per the goal orientation of the agency organising the training programme.

Training dilemma

Whatever the emphasis, every training programme has to confront certain dilemmas which exercises a determining influence on the specifics of organisational approaches such as duration, content, methodology. These dilemmas can be identified as follows:

(i) *Theory versus practice*: The training in social development obviously cannot be equated with one needed to master a material technology. Social development in its very nature involves social change at the individual, intstitutional and societal level in consistent and convergent manner. Any attempt at segmental as against integral change may bring about distortion or result in failure. As such theory practice relationship in all training programmes has to be judiciously balanced and dichotomy between the two is to be done away with. For, the accomplishment of training objectives critically depends as much on internalisation of a perspective which is the contribution of theory as on the acquisition of task-oriented skill which is the contribution of practice.

(ii) *Trainee versus task*: Another difficult option before training is whether to focus on the trainee himself or the task has to perform in the field. When there are several compulsions and pragmatic considerations, there is a tendency to highlight the task components in the training programme schedule. This is bound to militate against an authentic training philosophy, according to which the normative functions of all training should be to raise the problem-solving capacity of the trainee field worker and not directly solve his specific-problem which is difficult to visualise in the training situation.

(iii) *Structured versus unstructured*: Another equally perplexing dilemma is whether the training should be organised on the basis of a pre-structured programme-schedule or conducted in an unstructured manner making full allowance for self-perceived needs and requirements of the trainees. The logic in dictating and validating a structured programme emanates from a situation when time at the disposal of the training organiser has been tightly budgeted and the content area to be covered is definite and rather large. A structured programme emerging from the perceptions of the organiser is also supposed to have sequential order and systemic coherence which may better answer to the needs of the field functionaries. Be that us it may, the pre-structured programme in the ultimate analysis is an imposition unwelcome to the trainees. On the other hand, an unstructured programme has the merit of ensuring better trainee participation and the demerit of leading to inconsequential achievement.

(iv) *Acquisition versus application*: One more formidable problem, a training programme has to face is to be a very positively clear as to who should be the ultimate beneficiary of the training? The trainee may acquire a lot of information and knowledge and enrich his universe through training participation but if he does not apply his acquisitions as inputs to community welfare, the very rationale of the training goes astray. Therefore, though essential, it is found to be generally very difficult to build the application strategy into the planning structure of the training programme.

Establishment versus prochanges. When training is organised under government auspices 'establishment' philosophy acts as a great constraint on freedom of expression and experimentation. The rigid attitude of the establishment tends to ignore the coverage of a most critical component of development in raining i.e., structural change through a militant organisation of people an not through scientifically designed field programmes. Because of these constraints, the 'establishment' training is considered to have hardly succeeded by the activist group in accomplishing anything substantial so far as it concerns vital questions of social injustice, exploitation and oppression. Thus doubting the very legitimacy and efficacy of government training, the social activist groups have developed their own system of training broadly known as conscientisation.

Basic considerations

Whatever the auspices and whatever the type of training, a training programme in order to be effective has to follow some basic principles. These are:

(i) Training has to be viewed as an organic process of growth corresponding to dynamics of the field, the body of experiences constantly being generated all over and innovative project models developed by committed agencies in diverse fields and situations. In order to fully utilise the feedback from these sources, a training programme necessarily has to be flexible and multi-dimensional in its formal as well as substantive aspects.

(ii) The role of human factor in development has now been duly recognised as of crucial significance; training is no longer consider as an auxiliary or subsidiary component of development.

On the contrary, it has become the most potent instrument of contending groups to foster their own ideological and even vested interest, if the training organisers want to remain true to themselves, they must, therefore, guard themselves against the ulterior design of the sponsors and founders of a training programme.

Thus as the training task has assumed a new complexity of structure and organisation, it cannot be carried out successfully by a single organisation in isolation and insulation from others. It is now imperative that alienation among training, academic, administrative and specialised institutions should be done away with once for all, in order to promote a dynamic interaction among them through exchange of expertise, experiences, aids and equipment.

Now, no training institution can afford to sit in an ivory tower cut off from the grassroots level reality. In order, therefore, to maintain and augment the relevance of training, training institution either adopts the field as its laboratory for experimentation and innovation or exchanges regularly its academic personnel with field functionaries. This strategy is inevitable if training has to remain ever-vitalised, relevant and a rewarding enterprise.

Auspices of training

Training of functionaries is generally considered a prerequisite, while planning and implementing a programme/scheme. Normally, training programmes are conducted under the following auspices:

(i) Training centres under an autonomous institution set up under the control of the Government.

(ii) The responsibility of training entrusted to a university or an academic institution, and

(iii) A non-governmental agency handling training programmes.

Training under government set-up

Advantages

(i) It is easier to plan and conduct a training programme based on the specific methods and objectives of a programme or scheme.

(ii) It also facilitates organisation of practical training/ field placement.

(iii) Participants are likely to show more interest in their job training.

(iv) The trainers have the direct knowledge, experience and expertise of the administrative problems involved in the implementation of the programme. This could be narrated in a better way.

(v) The status of the programme is enhanced through active participation of higher level officials.

(vi) Trainees are better disciplined in observing the code of conduct of the training centre.

Disadvantages

(i) In a governmental set up, it is difficult to draw expertise, technical resources and aids from other organisations involved in similar type of training programme.

(ii) The training becomes mechanical routine and monotonous which leaves limited scope for the growth of the trainees.

(iii) There is a lack of flexibility in governmental set up which puts serious hurdles to make training lively and interesting.

(iv) Training may be for a specific job. Hence it may be narrow in content and scope.

Training under university set-up

One of the basic assumptions is that training is not only "knowing more" but is also for behaviour changes. The focus is not on information but on attitude, and skills. This contrasts with the academic, conformist and uncreative system of education generally prevailing which is based on the widespread myth that 'simply acquiring knowledge in the key to effective action.'

Advantages

(i) The purpose of such training is generally to disseminate information and to strengthen conceptual understanding.

(ii) One of the attractions is that it gives the trainers and trainees a respectable status of getting training of a higher standard.

(iii) The process of teaching and learning is predictable, as it remains under a teacher's control.

(iv) There is more flexibility in academic institutions than those prevailing in governmental set up.

(v) There is greater possibility of pooling of expertise from other departments of the university.

(vi) The academic institutions have also experience and expertise of training.

Disadvantages

(i) Lecture is its characteristic method and appraisal is by means of examinations, usually written.

(ii) The usual approach is that content and understanding can be passed from those who know to those who are ignorant.

(iii) The programme may tend to become purely academic.

(iv) There may not be sufficient financial, administrative and other support from the government which may hamper the training programme.

(v) The present day indiscipline prevailing in an Indian university may adversely affect quality of training.

(vi) Universities have also become bureaucratic and hence less flexible.

Training under non-governmental agencies

Training under non-governmental agencies is mostly imparted to enhance the practical skills. Mainly, voluntary agencies assume that whatever a trainee learns will be sufficient to allow him to deal not only with the requirements of his jobs but also with the new and unexpected roles.

Advantages

(i) Flexibility of work in non-governmental organisations may be useful.

(ii) Non-governmental organisations may be able to provide field-based experience to trainees.

(iii) It is possible to invite resource persons from other agencies.

Disadvantages

(i) Training imparted to participants may not be relevant to the job requirement of trainees.

(ii) Training may also sometimes lack the necessary academic input.

(iii) Staff may lack administrative experiences and its identification with trainees may not be possible as staff may not be taken into consideration seriously by trainees.

(iv) It may also be difficult to attract suitably qualified and experienced faculty.

(v) There may not be discipline among trainees as the agency code of conduct may lack administrative support for its enforcement.

(vi) Such training may be suitable and effective only for less skilled jobs.

(vii) It may not add status to a training programme especially when the training agency is not well-known.

(viii) The institution may also not be able to succeed in getting adequate support from resource persons of government departments, universities or high academic institutions.

Approaches to training

There are several approaches to training—conventional and innovative.

Informative

One of the approaches to the training is giving information on the subject-matter concerning the trainees. For instance, child development worker needs information about the growth and development, milestones in the early life of a baby, principles of growth, various basic services necessary for the growth and development of the child. Normally this information is a part of the syllabus of students of child development/nutrition in a Home Science College, and family and child welfare in the schools of social work. This information has to be imparted normally to the trainees who, by and large, do not possess it. In passing this information to them again conventional classroom method or chalk and talk method is generally used.

Even in giving information, one need not confine to conventional classroom 'chalk and talk' method. There should be use of other increasing, innovative or effective methods of imparting information through various teaching aids.

Participatory

Another non-traditional approach which is now commonly being used in the training programme is participatory approach. In this method, the trainer only becomes a leader or a helper in selecting a leader from the group itself who initiates the topic through a variety of ways and the trainees are encouraged to seek and give information based on their own experience, ask questions, give comments on the skills already presented. In this process, the trainer also learns from the experience of the trainees which he pools for their benefit. The participatory method is considered the most effective method of training. This has been dealt with in more detail in the ensuing chapter.

Experimental

There is yet another approach known as experimental approach, which involves direct experience of a highly personal nature in addition to sensitivity. This approach relates directly to the trainees. Under this approach, the trainees are helped to share experiences on different programmes, projects and services. This method applies more effectively in providing training to those who have some field experience.

Types of training

The training could be organised through the following:

(a) a well-structured course

(b) placement in an institution

(c) workshop

(d) seminar

In addition to a structured training course, placement, workshops, seminars and conferences would also become instruments of training, with reference to orientation of a functionary to a particular programme or field of activity.

Forms of training

There are certain other forms of training. These are as under:

(i) A fully structured training programme which may normally be in the classroom situation.

(ii) There may be semi-structured training programme in which the bulk of the structuring, if any, is left to the trainees.

(iii) There may be a totally unstructured training programme.

(iv) A course which is based primarily on job placement from the very beginning.

(i) Structured training programme

The system of structuring a training programme is derived from the formal education system. It is, therefore, a more commonly used form of training. In the structured training programme, the syllabus and the daily programme schedule are drawn by the training institution as they consider relevant to the needs of the trainees and different topics are covered under a stipulated time-frame. Such courses are generally planned well in advance, where the experts also share their views and experiences with the trainees on different topics.

Even in structured training programmes, the programme schedule may be discussed with the trainees after registration and initial orientation, so that the personal group needs of the trainees could be taken into consideration before finalising the programme. Accordingly, there may be changes in the programme schedule. Some new topics may be added, while some topics may be deleted or modified. This may also involve adding some names to the list of guest faculty. Changes in respect of observational visits, practicals, field work may laos be necessitated suiting to changing requirement.

Drawbacks

(i) The emphasis in the programmes is mainly on dissemination of information.

(ii) The contents of the programme are to be rigidly followed.

(iii) There is only one trainer responsible for the programme who may be called Course/Programme Direct.

(iv) Sometimes, the trainers do not possess adequate training or expertise in using innovative methods and aids relevant to training situations.

(v) Several outside conventional resource persons are invited in the programme for short durations. It becomes difficult for them to dovetail their expertise suiting to requirements of training programmes.

(vi) Trainers have to maintain a very rigid attitude.

(vii) Adequate importance is not accorded to self-awareness and attitudes of the trainees in the training programme.

(viii) Facilities for practical and field visits are not always available.

(ix) Coverage of the syllabus during a specified time becomes the most important objective for the training institutions.

(ii) Semi-structured training programme

A semi-structured training programme is formulated with basic assumptions that necessary changes are made as and when required based on the needs of the trainees. Although effort is made in the beginning of the course, 'to consult' the trainees, yet it appears to be only a formality. Immediately after a trainee registers himself/herself, he/she is not in a position to react to the training programme to the extent necessary. Therefore, this kind of semi-structured programme is also not very effective.

In this approach, it will be useful to develop and finalise the programme-schedule along with the trainees.

However, there may be difference of opinion, particularly if the group is heterogeneous. The other method would be to start with a structured programme which is in the nature of orientation to the subject. Later, when the participants are fully acquainted with the training exercises, they could be consulted for developing the training schedule/model. However, proper leadership of the trainer of the course/programme director is very important in this regard.

(iii) Unstructured training programme

The unstructured training programme is a very recent innovation in training technology. However, this is the most difficult method of technology. However, this is the most difficult method of training. This model calls for maturity and necessary skills by the trainees. Under the model, the trainees themselves structure the day-to-day programme, as there is no pre-structured programme. The trainers have to do considerable hard work in a programme like this as they play a crucial role. However, the objectives of the programme must be very clear both to the trainers and the trainees. Before the trainees are involved in the planning of the programme, it should be made known to them what the organisers intend to ultimately achieve through an unstructured training programme. It may be remembered that unstructured training programme can be organised only if a group is manageable from the point of view of a number of participants or trainees. It calls for tremendous initiative, innovation and hardwork on the part of the trainers in mobilizing the resources in terms of manpower, teaching methods, teaching aids, reading material, practicals, field work placement etc.

Prerequisites of an unstructured programme

(i) The trainers should possess sufficient maturity, experience and skills.

(ii) The objective of the programme is clear to the trainees as well as trainers.

(iii) The organisers and the trainees are prepared to explore and venture into innovative areas.

(iv) Necessary resources are made available to the group as and when the programme develops at short notice.

(v) The trainers have a sense of patience and an attitude of wait and watch.

(vi) The trainers are prepared to forgo wastage of resources in an unstructured programme.

(iv) Job training

The job or inservice training or refresher courses may be structured for classroom type of instructions, while orientation course may be in the nature of a seminar or a conference or a workshop, Seminar or a workshop is a method of training which is utilized for orientation of the senior officers who are unable to take advantage of classroom trailing programme. Apart from classroom type of training courses with practicals or field visits, there may be other types of training such as on the job training or apprenticeship. A detailed description of these are given below. From the point of view of its relationship with job performance and time sequence in the career of a functionary the training is of different kinds.

1. Pre-service training

Pre-service training is generally in the nature of university level professional educational or specialised training for functionaries before they are appointed in different jobs. By and large, pre-service training is organised by the universities and other professional and technical institutions of learning such as schools of social work, home science colleges, medical colleges.

The difference between pre-service and in-service training is that the latter is organised after a functionary is duly recruited and offered a job. As a prerequisite for the job, he/she undergoes, in-service training or on the job training. Pre-service training is in the nature of education given to a person for a specific job, so that he stands in a queue along with others to compete for a job on the basis of pre-service training. This pre-service training may be organised as part of the regular curriculum of universities or may be done by government, voluntary and academic institutions.

In-service training programme is of specified duration. The idea is that during the training period, the trainee is able to acquire necessary skills for his job which he is going to utilise in work situations. In fact, in-service training programme is conceived because the personnel who are recruited do not necessarily have the background to discharge their role and responsibilities in job situations. For example, if the minimum qualifications such as M.Sc. in Child Development, M.A. in Social Work etc., for appointment of the Child Development Project Officers was adhered to, there would not be need for longer in-service training for them. If the pre-service training was insisted upon, in-service training of a shorter duration could be some kind of orientation to the programme.

The duration of the training programme varies from programme to programme and functionary to functionary. In the context of ICDS, the duration of the training programme for different functionaries is as under:

Anganwadi workers : Four months
Supervisors : Three months
Child Development
Project Officers : Eight weeks
Orientation of higher

level functionaries : One week through seminars or workshops

2. Induction vs. in-service training

Sometimes, there is confusion between induction training and in-service training as many do not see any difference between the two. The UN Handbook of Training in Public Service says "inservice training of public employees may be distinguished from the pre-entry preparation by reference to two test, namely, the time at which the training is given and the nature and content of instruction."

A suitable distinction is also necessary between in-service and job training. For every job, certain minimum educational and professional qualifications are required in addition to some minimum field experience. Therefore, even if the person is fully qualified by virtue of educational/professional background he/she would require some training and field experience which in other words could mean orientation to the job—understanding the objectives, contents, organisational structure, budgeting pattern, funding system, monitoring, evaluation of the programme on which she/he has to work.

A job training which requires the functionary to undertake the job is also equated with in-service training. Therefore, there is difference in details between the induction training and in-service training. These cannot be planned in the same manner and at the same time.

Job-training course

The Government has launched several programmes of development from time to time such as those of community development, welfare extension projects, family and child welfare, Integrated Child Development Services. For these programmes, the Government recruited a large number of functionaries at different levels with varied backgrounds and organised in-service training for them. By and large, there are four levels of these functionaries.

(i) Grassroot level functionaries working at the village level such as *Gramsevikas, Balsevikas, Anganwadi* workers, Adult Education Instructors, House mothers, Health Guides etc. some of whom are also honorary workers.

(ii) Supervisory or middle level functionaries such as, Mukhyasevikas of Community Developments, supervisors of Child Development, Lady Health Visitors.

(iii) Officers at the project or block level such as Block Development Officers, Medical Officers, of primary health centres, the Child Development Project Officers, Child Welfare Organisers of the Family Welfare Programme, Superintendents of Children's Institutions.

For all these functionaries, there has been system of job-training. A person having educational and professional qualification of a university or pre-university degree with some experience prescribed for job retirement has to undergo job training after recruitment. He is given training suited to the scheme or the programme which he/she is going to implement. The training centre staff is given orientation to the scheme which includes information on various topics concerning the scheme, skills necessary for running such a programme and attitudes.

Refresher training course

One of the basic needs of development-oriented programme for which in-service or job-training courses are designed is that of development information which may take place in the fields and new experiences based on feedback after in-service training. The refresher course is to be organised only for those who has the opportunity of being exposed to the job or in-service training course. Quite often, the refresher course is misconceived as a capsule job-training course. The refresher courses should not only review the various skills and methods used in earlier job training with reference to the field experiences of the trainers as well as trainees but also to deal with new skills and new areas of subject-matter. Refresher training also helps in revising the syllabus of the training. Ideally, the refresher course should be of a duration ranging from one week to ten days depending upon the level of the functionaries. In a refresher course, training methods should be innovative in nature. There should be an emphasis on job oriented practical training.

Orientation programme

Orientation programme is conducted for workers before they are put on the job in which they are given orientation in a particular field or activity. In other words, the orientation is to the job and the field situations to which workers' are going to be exposed. For instance, a child care worker who has the requisite qualifications M.Sc., M.S.W., could be given orientation to the programme of child development in which they are going to be placed. The orientation programme presupposes that the person has the knowledge and the skills of the subject-matter. An orientation programme may be generally of one week's duration.

Seminar-workshop

Other informal forms of training are seminars and workshops covering a particular topic or issue but not the whole field of activities. Such techniques are useful and are taken advantage of by senior policy-makers, board members, officers, planners and professionals who because of age, status, lack of spare time, motivation and other reasons are unable to participate in formal training programmes. These forms of training have been discussed in more detail in the chapter on Training Methods.

Other forms of training

The training covers the following areas;

(i) Attitude or personal development training
(ii) Skill training
(iii) Field training

Such training programmes of innovative nature are organised by a limited number of training agencies which have sufficient experience in these areas.

There are a number of other activities, of significant training value, which can be organised or encouraged within an agency possibly with the help of training establishments. These activities include:

(a) broadening experience for members of staff whose experience in an agency been largely restricted to a specialised field and who may need experience in a number of departments;

(b) individual or group projects—these call for carrying out of a specific well-defined task, either by one individual operating in different sections or departments or by a group drawn from several departments dealing with a common problem. Project work has proved to be a valuable alternative to departmental attachments, but it should always be carefully planned and supervised. The results should also be discussed fully with the participants. A project is often useful as a means of practising recently acquired techniques in real situations;

(c) participation in meetings, conferences and lectures

both within the agency or as part of the activities of professional organisations. These are valuable as a means of keeping abreast with new ideas and developing standards of comparison;

(d) short courses, discussions or talks within the agencies on subjects relevant to the job of the trainees.

Review of training

During the last thirty-five years of the process of development in India, several methods and techniques and types of training have been adopted with reference to implementing developmental programmes. India has the expertise of organising massive country-wide programmes of training in Community Development and Child Development. It was always the Central Government which provided leadership and wherewithals for training in various national programmes like community development, social welfare, health, education and child development. The officers have been exposed to the in-service or job training course of duration varying from one month to one year. Because of problems of logistics and the size of the country, the trainees are required to travel longer distances to come to the training centres. This is also because of the institutionalised nature of training.

Thereafter, in many cases it has not been possible because of various reasons to bring the trainees back to the training centres to help the trainers in the training centres to understand their problems and the needs of the workers in the field, so that the next training programme could be improved. Nor are they brought back for refresher course, although, there have been attempts in modifying the training curriculum, learning methods, teaching aids, field work system etc. This is based on the feedback which the trainers themselves got when they visited the field objects. There has not been a process of continuous interaction between the trainers and the trainees in field situations after they have been trained. Sometimes there may be written communications from the trainees and vice versa but this again happens very rarely.

11

Recent Developments in Training

The training methods and techniques have been developed in various forms, frequently being modified and tailored to suit particular situations and needs. The profession is, of course, constantly evolving, and training specialists seek to take advantage of any new technologies, methods or approaches which may promise to add to their effectiveness. Often what is offered as innovative is readily recognizable as something from the past simply dressed up in a new guise and described in a new jargon. Training staff should therefore be on their guard against offers of 'new' developments which may only treat them to 'the mixture as before', possible laced with a new flavour.

In a number of areas, training can be justly said to be breaking new ground. While the foundations for such developments may have been laid some years ago, it is only Now, in the mid-1980s, that we can see real progress being made. In a rapidly changing world, one can only take a snapshot of what is happening at the time of writing and this could well be out of date in a matter of months. Specialists developing new ideas may sensibly resist telling the world about their activities until there is adequate evidence that their worth can be demonstrated.

The following are the areas in which training would appear to be making some progress currently:

Computer-based training

It was briefly mentioned in the last chapter that the use of computer-based training (CBT) adds a valuable dimension in speeding up decision-making and so compressing the training time-scale. In recent years, micro-technology has contributed to reductions in the cost of computer hardware, opening up opportunities for promoting its use in the training area. Only a few years ago the cost of the computer equipment itself was beyond the means of the training department; most of today's cost is in the program of software.

Facilities for accessing programs may be provided by large computers, which are operated on a time-sharing basis, or by micro-computer. Time-sharing requires a link-up of the terminal a remote computer by telephone line. Difficulties may arise from unsuitable siting of the computer, unfavourable priorities, response delays of equipment breakdown. Sometimes it is possible to limit some of these problem by arranging the use of a computer exclusively for training purposes through a computer bureau. The micro-computer, however, has a distinct advantage over other systems: it offers a comprehensive facility on one's own premises. Computer, terminals and display units can all be accommodated in a limited amount of office space and the complete system is under the user's control. All that is required is a modest electrical power source and suitable programs or software. The training department thus has immediate access to a valuable facility which provides both versatility and portability.

Computer technology in business is now a fact of life, being increasingly used in the larger organizations where the implementation and running costs are more readily justified and absorbed. Smaller businessmen, however, are included to show reluctance to take advantage of new technological developments, not only from the point of view of economics but also because they are apprehensive about being caught up in activities which they do not fully understand. Indeed as entrepreneurs who have been used to holding the business reins and taking all the decisions themselves, they feel that there is a risk that technology could take over completely. It is an important responsibility of members of the training profession to reassure them on this point. The managers need to be shown by non-technical people who do not have a vested commercial interest in the equipment itself that the computer is not something which will take over their thought processes or their jobs, but will only do what they command it to do. In this respect, its obedience may outshine that of some of their employees.

What can training specialists achieve by using computers in their own work? The MSC has urged employers who introduce new technology into their organizations to ensure that they make full use of the computer's teaching and training potential. As with all training media, there must be a pay-off in terms of improved performance at economic cost, so it is logical to assess their applications against this criterion. For some years computers were seen as sophisticated calculators rather than as aids to decision-making. It is true that their facility for producing phenomenally rapid and accurate results where complex mathematics is concerned is of considerable importance. The removal of the drudgery in repetitive arithmetical tasks is certainly welcomed. More recently, however, many other training applications have developed which enable computer technology to make more significant contributions to organizational effectiveness, with the added benefit of economies of scale. The more important of these applications are listed below:

Management of training

The activities of planning, organizing, monitoring, assessing, recording etc. are assumed to involve manual systems. All are extremely time-consuming and some can be quite complicated. Professional training managers who see the trainer or instructor role as the most important part of their jobs are only too pleased to be able to delegate as many of the organizing activities as possible to their supporting staff. The computer can be an extremely useful tool in controlling and speeding up these activities, thus reducing the administrative burden.

There are several ways in which computer programs can be helpful in the management of training. In a large organization the planning of the department's activities and the management of all its resources, such as instructors, training rooms, equipment, training materials, stationery, can involve the control of a large number of variables. This is not always handled as efficiently as it should be and frequently becomes a fire-fighting exercise. Resources are allocated arbitrarily as the need arises and without regard for the effects such action creates elsewhere. A properly designed computer program can take the guesswork out of such decisions, planning the disposition of resources and providing an instant appraisal of their availability.

A trainee's progress through the system can also be more efficiently traced by the computer than by the more common manual means. Details of his educational and occupational background may be stored in the database ready to be retrieved at any time they may be required. This record can also include reports on his training progress, whether as part of a continuing programme or resulting from single modules of training such as technical updating. His future training needs can be fed into the system and the program designed to provide information on the most suitable means of satisfying them. Clearly, a program which provides such detailed data on all the employees trained or under training can also become the source of valuable statistics about the whole training activity in a given period.

Learning aid

The facilities are now being exploited to the full and enable much more sophisticated programs to be designed. To date programmed learning has in effect simulated the page of a book, with a provision for student responses and for revision where the answers given are incorrect. The statements made and questions asked are standard and inflexible. The latest development of a so-called Socratic method in which a more natural dialogue can take place between man and machine. This has led some people to credit the computer with human 'intelligence'. In fact it simply requires a more complex program, which of course demands the employment of more highly skilled programmers.

There have been some interesting new developments in the use of computers in simulations, too. Greg Kearsley, in his informative book *Computer-Based Training,* describes a novel method of training technicians in troubleshooting and repairing electronic circuitry. Circuit diagrams are displayed on the screen and a light pen is used by the trainee to measure to measure voltages at different points in the circuit. When faults are diagnosed, 'repairs' are effected by means of the light pen, this time employed as a 'soldering iron'.

Information source for trainees

There is nothing new in using a computer as a source of information. It is capable of storing a considerable quantity of data. With the increasing preoccupation of trainers with the concept of trainee-based learning, however, it is not surprising that this facility is being used more and more. Learners carrying out training tasks are able to access the information they need through suitable programs in the training room and elsewhere. The computer database provided by MARIS for the Open Tech programme can provide them with detailed information about open learning materials available.

Design of training programmes

Just as scientists and engineers can make use of computer-aided design when developing new concepts and products, so trainers can enlist the help of computers when designing their training programmers. The system lends itself to a high degree of experimentation with various ideas and approaches, with the advantage of instant modification where found necessary.

The discipline required in producing a computer program for particular training application encourages precision in terminology and presentation which may not be present when designing a training programme manually. There is a temptation when writing course materials in the traditional way to be unnecessarily unwieldy in the choice and use of language, making the process more complicated than it need be. The result could well be that the trainees become bored and consequently demotivated. Furthermore, the use of graphical and pictorial representation may not normally be fully exploited, because of the inordinate amount of time necessary to produce something acceptable. A computerized design system, if it does not entirely eliminate such problems, goes a long way towards reducing them. An enormous amount of potential training data can also be stored for retrieval as and when required. Searching for specific information in the database takes a fraction of the time needed to work through books and filing cabiners.

The degree of complexity of a computer program suitable for course design raises an important question. The trainer's own training and experience will have concentrated essentially on putting information obtained from practitioners into a suitable learning form. In no way can he be knowledgeable about every aspect of the business likely to be encountered in training. It is probably asking too much that he should be trained in the intricacies of computer programming, which is considered to be a profession in its own right. This suggests that course design has to be a team effort. Detailed information on the topics to be explored has to be obtained from the practitioners, a computer specialist converts that information into a suitable program and the trainer ensures that appropriate training principles are observed and that the outcome meets the agreed objectives.

Testing

A common use of computer programs in training is for test purposes. This application is mentioned here not because it is in any sense a new development, but rather because it is sufficiently important to merit inclusion. For this reason, it is constantly under review and subject to change. As stated earlier, a computer program can provide the basis for assessing a trainees' progress; that is, it can be employed to measure his performance against certain criteria. Those criteria can be incorporated into the program and the computer can carry out the laborious task of comparing performance of a number of trainees against them. The program can also be designed in such a way that it provides a means of selection for training, thus avoiding expensive mistakes in allowing trainees to embark on training programmes to which they are not suited.

By entering appropriate data into the database, tests

or exercises may be devised. The correct answers are identified in the program and the accuracy of the trainee's responses communicated either to the trainee himself or to the trainer, as desired. Again, the use of pictorial representation has increased the sophistication of such tests, which do not have to be restricted to the written word. Pictures or diagrams may be used to rest a trainees' capacity to identify certain objects, e.g. an electronic component or sub-assembly which has been shown elsewhere simply by means of symbols.

The flexibility of testing by computer is demonstrated by one of the more advanced forms of interactive testing, known as adaptive testing. Although the program may contain a large number of items designed to test a trainee's comprehension of certain principles, it is not necessary for him to work through all of them or even to satisfy them sequentially in order to demonstrate his understanding. His responses to a limited number of questions will show whether or not he has grasped the appropriate concepts to satisfy given training objectives. The process of testing can thus be speeded up considerably and can proves less frustrating for the trainee.

When evaluating a training programme, for example by the use questionnaires, the collation and interpretation of information from a number of trainees can be an onerous task. Clearly the computer can not only lighten the load by reducing the sheer volume of work, but can also be programmed to interpret the results more meaningfully by drawing attention to the interrelationships between certain responses.

Embedded training

One of the obvious applications of the computer is providing a program which teaches the learner how to use the equipment. Over ten years ago the writer adopted this device on a computerized sales forecasting course. The sales trainees were given instruction through the computer terminal on how to program the computer in the BASIC language. This had the dual advantage of concurrently teaching them about the system and giving them practice in using it. Nowadays it is common practice for suppliers of computer equipment, word processors etc. to include embedded training in the contract of supply.

Do we need computer-based training?

From the above it may be felt that computer-based training (CBT) has a good deal to offer the training manager. Only the salesman is likely to want to convince him that it will provide all the answers to his training problems. It is dangerous, however, to assume that since it is based on new and ever-advancing technology it has to be good. It is equally wrong to avoid trying to evaluate it because it requires radical re-thinking which is somewhat daunting. Some training specialists will be inclined to evade the question by pleading that the cost of implementing CBT would be prohibitive. An honest and detailed appraisal of the alternative means of satisfying an organization's precise training needs is the only way of providing the evidence to support or contest this view. In some businesses, the introduction of CBT has saved money; in others it has cost more than was expected. How does one calculate the cost? If the system is more expensive in hard cash terms but leads to much greater efficiency and effectiveness, is this not an argument for considering it seriously?

It is not at all easy to compare the two alternatives. So much depends on how well the training operation is being carried out without the assistance of the computer. Simply computerizing a sub-standard performance at a higher level of skill, and failure may have more far-reaching effects. For example, in a process industry, the whole costly operation may be brought to a standstill and people and plant put at risk by a single person failing to note and take action on changing conditions in his particular sector. Repetitive manual skills may thus have to be replaced by skills requiring a more intelligent approach to work of a non-recurring nature. An analysis of all possible causes of employee error has to be made in order to provide training which will adequately fit employees for these new tasks. The approach to operator training outlined above goes a long way towards easing the transition from a repetitive manual job to a monitoring or controlling one. If the employee really understands his job, he will more readily see the reasons for change and be more likely to go along with it.

Apprentice training changes

The traditional method of training craftsmen by indentured apprenticeship is rapidly disappearing. The concept of an indenture, a contract 'that binds apprentice to master' and which originally had to be paid for by the unfortunate parents, is an anachronism the removal of which is long overdue. Many 'masters' clung to the idea that the apprentice needed to serve at least five years, i.e. until he reached the age of discretion at 21, before he could be considered suitably skilled to carry out a craftsman's or production worker's job without supervision. Learning by experience in this way was a very long drawn-out affair and depended for its success on the level of instructional skill of the craftsman alongside whom the apprentice worked and on the latter's determination to complete the apprenticeship and 'take up' his indentures. The advances in training philosophy and methods in the years since the war, stimulated partly by the recommendations of the Industrial Training Boards and the Engineering Council, have gradually made the apprenticeship concept redundant. It is now in process of being replaced by 'training agreements'.

The indenture agreement was a remarkably 'open' document. It specified the length of the apprenticeship precisely, but frequently said little, if anything, about what training the apprentice could expect. In spite of this vagueness, the skilled worker who could wave his indentures in front of an employer was more likely to get a job than one who could not. It was proof that he had completed a programme of training as, for example, a miller or turner, but it seldom identified the skills learned or the standards attained. By contrast, the training agreement is more likely to indicate that induction training, basic skills training, specified skills modules and a part-time course of further education have to be completed to acceptable standards before the agreement may be said to have been discharged. The number and type of skills modules are usually agreed by management and union before the programme is commenced and a statement is made to the effect that the duration will depend upon how long the trainee takes to satisfy the requirements of the various modules.

The implications of these changes for the trainee are self-evident. He knows from the start of a training programme exactly what is going to be required of him, which may allay any fears that he may be used as cheap labour. The training itself will have to be more relevant, because the requirements of each module will have to be satisfied and suitably certificated before he can move on to the next one. This should help to ensure that he is given instruction on skills which are essential, with less attention to those which are simply 'nice to knew'. There are also advantages in his not having to sit out a four-or five-year apprenticeship when he may be quite capable of acquiring the necessary skills in three years. The employer is bound to benefit also. Apart from producing a skilled worker earlier, the standard of training itself is predictably higher, with consequent effects on the quality of output. If the trainee has enjoyed the acquisition of new skills to a high standard within a reasonable period of time and there have been fewer frustrations along the line, it is reasonable to expect him to be better motivated.

Instructional systems development

Training systems fail to meet their objectives for a variety of reasons. The materials may be deficient in important features or may provide too much information of the wrong kind. When training does not meet its objectives of teaching the skills required by employees to carry out their tasks effectively, there is cause for concern. There are also problems of consistency, for example when training manpower resources are supplemented by the part-time use of non-training specialists with appropriate 'technical' knowledge. They may not be familiar with training techniques or the production of training materials, with the result that they develop their own, sometimes in conflict with the training department's philosophy.

A technique known as Instructional Systems Development (ISD) may be helpful in dealing with such problems and others by providing a co-ordinated approach to the training system as a whole. It tabulates what steps have to be taken in each stage of the training process. It does not, however, detail how these steps should be carried out. Nonetheless, most training managers appreciate having checklists to guide them in their activities and ISD fulfils that need in so far as it provides them with prompts in working through the training system and developing training materials.

The various stages in the ISD approach used by the

American services will already be familiar to training staff:

- *analysis* - training needs are derived in relation to the requirements of each task of job. Appropriate performance criteria are established.
- *design* - objectives are defined, structure and sequencing determined, tests devised
- *development* - learning media and methods are selected and training materials developed
- *implementation* - the instructional plan is put into effect
- *control* - the programmes are evaluated and the system modified as necessary.

Some of the activities in the above stages are interrelated. For instance, evaluation is something which is taking place all the time and is not simply confined to the control stage. In the event of the training failing to meet the established objectives, it may be necessary to return to the analysis stage and re-start the process.

As will be clear from the earlier section on computer-based systems, there is considerable scope for the use of computers in conjunction with ISD. While it applies to all stages of the process, the areas where it has created greatest interest have been in the design and evaluation of training materials and in testing.

Index